Patrick O'Neill is a member of the Department of Germanic Studies at the University of British Columbia. He is also the author of *Günter Grass: A Bibliography 1955-1975*.

This volume provides an accessible, up-to-date, select bibliography of the major works of German authors available in book form in English. The primary basis for selection has been that of literary excellence, with secondary importance placed on cultural interest. Therefore, 'popular' writing without high literary standards has been in general excluded, as have the writings of philosophers, historians, anthropologists, and the like, except where they are considered to have literary merit in their own right. This bibliography is enumerative rather than critical or evaluative, and contains only 'modern' translations, that is to say primarily twentieth-century translations or twentieth-century reprints of older translations where the enduring excellence of the latter has been generally recognized or where no later translation exists. Covering the period up to the end of 1979, the entries include authors of all periods and are divided into five parts: general collections; all writings prior to 1700; and writings of the eighteenth, nineteenth, and twentieth centuries respectively. Within the individual sections entries are arranged alphabetically by author or in the case of anonymous works by original title.

This volume is particularly useful for teachers in the humanities, especially those in German and comparative literature.

German Literature
in English Translation

A SELECT BIBLIOGRAPHY

PATRICK O'NEILL

UNIVERSITY OF TORONTO PRESS

Toronto Buffalo London

© University of Toronto Press 1981

Toronto   Buffalo   London

Printed in Canada

ISBN 0-8020-2409-2

Canadian Cataloguing in Publication Data

O'Neill, Patrick, 1945-
German literature in English translation

Includes indexes.
ISBN 0-8020-2409-2

1. German literature - Translations into English -
Bibliography.   2. English literature - Translations
from German - Bibliography.   I. Title.

Z2234.T7053   016.83   C81-094561-4

BE
4-26-82

Contents

Preface

The following listing grew out of practical rather
than theoretical considerations: a decade or so of
teaching courses in German literature in translation persuaded me of the need for an up-to-date
and readily accessible bibliography of those works
of major German authors available in book form in
English. The primary usefulness of the listing,
therefore, I believe, will be for the teaching
scholar in the humanities, the student of comparative literature, and the educated general reader
rather than the literary statistician. The listing
reflects my personal conception of what the canon
of German literature (as available in translation)
is at the beginning of the 1980s, my impression of
what is best, most lasting, and most interesting to
the English-speaking reader who has a taste for
literature. That impression is of course contest-
able, as is the whole principle of selection.
Clearly there are objections to such a prescriptive
canon of literature; clearly the canon will have
changed appreciably in fifty or even twenty years'
time; clearly there are arguments for the inclusion
of detective stories, science fiction tales, crime
dramas, schoolgirl romances, and the whole gamut of
paraliterature. In practical terms, however, I
believe that my assumptions are those of a very
large number of educated readers.

A select bibliography, of course, is useful only
in direct proportion to the good judgment of the com-
piler, who, like the anthologist of literary works,
exposes himself to the wrath alike of those outraged
by the exclusion of a favourite author and those
irritated by the inclusion of other authors of
obviously ephemeral interest. After several years of
intermittent mulling over the exclusion or inclusion
of this or that marginal author I can only hope that

I have offended more on the side of generosity,
without having reached such levels of warmhearted-
ness as would compromise the principle of selection.
The basis for selection throughout has been literary
excellence in the first place and cultural interest
in the second, with very much less emphasis on the
latter. 'Popular' writing without high literary
standards has been in general excluded, as have the
writings of philosophers, historians, anthropologists, and the like, unless they are generally considered to have clear literary merit in their own
right. In a few such cases--Freud and Jung, for
example--for reasons of cultural interest a compromise has been attempted in that the standard English
translation of the author's complete works is listed
while other translations are not.

It is perhaps desirable to emphasize at the out-
set the fundamental difference between this listing
and the bibliographies of Bayard Quincy Morgan, which
have dominated this field for well over half a century. Morgan's monumental and magnificent *Bibliography of German literature in English translation*
was first published by the University of Wisconsin
Press, in 1922, and ran even then to over 7000
entries. Further editions in 1938 and 1965 hugely
augmented this original coverage, until eventually
Morgan was attempting not only to list but also to
evaluate *all* English translations of German literature which were published between 1481 and 1955.
The term 'literature', moreover, was interpreted
elastically to include such materials as philosophical works of Kant and Hegel, opera libretti,
collections of letters of famous Germans, and even
biographies. A supplement for the five-year period
1956-60, published in 1969 by Morgan's protégé
M.F. Smith, further extended the interpretation of
'literature' to include almost everything printed
in German.

Morgan's undertaking, deserving of all praise, was
one of enormous magnitude, and remains indispensable
for any investigation of the English-language re-
ception of German literature. Especially in the
later volumes, however, its rapidly increasing scope
tended to make it ever more unwieldy, and a very
large proportion of its bulk, as Morgan himself wrily

admitted, was made up of unreadable translations of
originals which were themselves of no conceivable
interest to anyone but the literary statistician.
To put it bluntly, though with all respect: the comprehensiveness of Morgan's listing in the end detrac-
ted rather than otherwise from its usefulness for the
reader who was primarily interested in establishing
the availability of readable English versions of the
major works of German literature. As for any translations which had appeared after 1960, the would-be
reader could turn to Richard Mönnig's *Translations
from the German* (1968) for publications until 1964.
Thereafter, however, he was forced to search such
periodical publications as the *British national
bibliography* or the Library of Congress subject
listings, an arduous and time-consuming task. Within
its chosen limits of selection and for its intended
audience the present listing makes consultation of
both Morgan and the huge national bibliographies
unnecessary for other than specialist purposes.

Other than scope and comprehensiveness, the main
methodological difference between this listing and
Morgan's is that the present listing is purely
enumerative, while Morgan's is critical and evaluative. This may disappoint some users of the present
listing, so a word of explanation is in order. My
main objective in compiling the bibliography was to
indicate availability rather than quality. Indeed
I have serious doubts as to the merits of a system
such as that employed by Morgan, where a one-word
verdict lauds a translation of five or six hundred
pages as 'excellent' or condemns it as 'poor'. A
procedure such as this undoubtedly has value in
dealing with translations dating from the fifteenth
to the nineteenth centuries, where translations were
frequently appallingly bad, frequently capricious
reworkings of the hapless original. The present
listing, however, unlike Morgan's, does not contain
translations of such vintages. On principle it
contains only 'modern' translations, that is to say
primarily twentieth-century translations or twentieth-
century reprints of older translations where the
enduring excellence of the latter has been generally
recognized or where no later translation exists. We
live in a golden age of translation, standards are
infinitely higher than before 1900, and the need for

evaluative bibliographies of translations corres-
pondingly less. I am not maintaining, of course,
that evaluation of translations is no longer neces-
sary, or that some translations are not inevitably
better than others. I am suggesting, however, that
one-word evaluations no longer suffice.

Finally, in this context, it should be unnecessary to point out that this listing in no way competes
with those trade publications which indicate the
current availability of a particular title. Users
who wish to establish whether a particular translation is still or again in print must turn as
before to such aids as *Books in print*, *British books
in print*, and *Paperback books in print*.

Because of the selectivity of the listing it is
not suited to serve as a basis for statistically
oriented investigations, or indeed as a springboard
here for a discussion of translation trends during the
twentieth century--any such investigation or discussion would have to take into account the vast
amounts of paraliterary, subliterary and quasi-
literary material which are also translated but are
left out of consideration here. Within the area of
selection coverage is as complete as I could make
it until the end of 1979. Authors of all periods
are represented, from the Middle Ages to the present
day, twentieth-century authors being particularly
strongly represented--which serves in broad terms as
an indication of one modern translation trend. The
period before 1700 is represented by some 150 entries,
the eighteenth century by some 200, the nineteenth
century by almost 500, and the twentieth century by
almost 1000, or more than all the rest together.
These proportions are not imposed, but derive na-
turally from the available material. In numerical
terms the chief focus of the listing is thus on English versions of recent and contemporary German
writing. In the earlier periods, however, sterling
work has also been done in recent years, and the
listing here should alleviate considerably the no-
torious difficulty, for example, of locating modern
and trustworthy versions of German texts dating from
before 1700.

The listing contains only translations which
have appeared in book form; translations appearing in

journals, newspapers, and elsewhere were excluded. The main sources searched for the listing were the *British national bibliography* from 1950, the Library of Congress subject catalogues from 1950, the *Index translationum* from 1965, and Morgan, Smith, and Mönnig for the earlier periods. Additional sources of varying usefulness were the trade listings of books in print, the periodical listing of German texts in English translation in *Unterrichtspraxis*, bibliographies and critical studies of individual authors, and publishers' catalogues. These sources vary considerably both in method and in accuracy of information. Where feasible entries were physically verified; but this was not always feasible, and mistakes have doubtless crept in; for these, like Johnson, I can only plead the excuse of ignorance, pure ignorance.

I follow the bibliographers of the Modern Language Association of America as to periodization, the first period covering all writings prior to 1700, further periods corresponding to the eighteenth, nineteenth, and twentieth centuries. Within the individual periods entries are arranged alphabetically by author, or, in the case of anonymous works, by original title. Authors whose creative output might be included in either or both of two periods are assigned to that period in which their major achievements may be said to lie--the relevant entries can in any case be quickly located by reference to the index of authors. Within the individual author entries items are arranged from the more general to the more specific: complete works and selections are listed first, followed by individual works listed alphabetically by their English titles. Since English titles of a particular work may vary considerably, cross-references have been provided where appropriate. The original title is listed in parentheses immediately after the English title in the individual entries. Bilingual editions are indicated as such. The abbreviation 'pb' indicates that a paperback version also exists--thus "New York: Grove Press, 1966, pb" indicates that Grove Press first published this particular translation in 1966 and that the work was also issued, then or subsequently, in paperback form.

My thanks are due to the Research Committee of the

University of British Columbia for generous finan-
cial aid, as also to the Canadian Federation for
the Humanities; to Norma Wieland for assistance in
searching; to Elizabeth Spence for preparing the
typescript; and to Trudi O'Neill, my wife and bib-
liographical widow, for toleration and forbearance.
The book has been published with the help of a grant
from the Canadian Federation for the Humanities,
using funds provided by the Social Sciences and
Humanities Research Council of Canada.

Patrick O'Neill
University of British Columbia
August, 1980

I General collection

1 BATES, Alfred, ed. *German drama*. New York: AMS Press, 1970 (1903), 3 vols.

    (I: Hans Sachs, Lessing, Schiller, Werner: II: Goethe, Iffland, Kotzebue, Benedix: III: Babo, Werner, Goethe, Hauptmann, Schnitzler).

2 BENEDIKT, Michael, and George Wellwarth, eds. and trans. *Postwar German theatre: An anthology*. New York: Dutton, 1967, pb; London: MacMillan, 1968.

    (Kaiser, The raft of the Medusa; Borchert, The outsider; Erwin Sylvanus, Dr. Korczak and the children; Dürrenmatt, Incident at twilight; Frisch, The great fury of Philip Hotz; Dorst, Freedom for Clemens; Carl Laszlo, Let's eat hair, The Chinese icebox; Grass, Rocking back and forth; Hildesheimer, Nightpiece; Peter Weiss, The tower).

3 BENJAMIN, Lewis, and Reginald Hargreaves. *Great German short stories*. London: Benn, 1929; Freeport, New York: Books for libraries Press, 1971.

4 BENNETT, E.N., ed. and trans. *German short stories*. London: Oxford University Press / The World's Classics, 1934.

    (Hoffmann, The mines of Falun; Kleist, The beggarwoman of Locarno; Tieck, Life's luxuries; Eichendorff, From the life of a good-for nothing; Droste-Hülshoff, The Jews' beech-tree).

5 BENTLEY, Eric, ed. *The classic theatre. Volume II:
Five German Plays. London: Mayflower Books: New York:
Doubleday, 1959, pb.

   (Goethe, Egmont; Schiller, Don Carlos, Mary Stuart;
   Kleist, Penthesilea, Prince of Homburg).

6 -----, ed. *From the modern repertoire: Series one.*
Denver: University of Denver Press, 1949; Bloomington:
Indiana University Press, 1956.

   (Includes: Brecht, The threepenny opera; Büchner,
   Danton's death; Schnitzler, Round dance; Sternheim,
   The snob).

7 -----, ed. *From the modern repertoire: Series two.*
Denver: University of Denver Press, 1952; Bloomington;
Indiana University Press, 1967.

   (Includes: Brecht, Galileo; Grabbe, Jest, satire,
   irony; Wedekind, The Marquis of Keith).

8 -----, ed. *From the modern repertoire: Series three.*
Bloomington: Indiana University Press, 1956, 1966.
   (Includes: Brecht, Saint Joan of the stockyards;
   Büchner, Leonce and Lena; Schnitzler, Anatol).

9 -----. *The great playwrights, volume 1.* Garden City,
N.Y.: Doubleday, 1970.
   (Includes: Kleist, Prince Frederick of Homburg;
   Brecht, Mother Courage, Caucasian chalk circle).

10 -----, ed. *The modern theatre.* New York: Doubleday/
Anchor, 1955-60, 6 vols. Gloucester, Mass.: P. Smith,
1974.

   (Includes: I; Büchner, Woyzeck; Brecht, Threepenny
   opera; II: Schnitzler, La ronde; V: Büchner, Danton's
   death; VI: Brecht, The measures taken; Wedekind,

BENTLEY, *The modern theatre* (cont'd).

Spring's awakening; Sternheim, The underpants).

11 BITHELL, Jethro, trans. *Contemporary German poetry.*
London, New York: Scott, 1909.

(Includes major selections from Bierbaum, Dauthendey, Dehmel, Lasker-Schüler, Liliencron, Miegel,
Mombert, Rilke, Hofmannsthal).

12 -----, ed. and trans. *The minnesingers. Volume I:
Translations.* London, New York: Longmans, 1909.

(Includes selections from: Kürenberg, Dietmar,
Veldeke, Friedrich von Hausen, Morungen, Reinmar,
Hartmann, Walther, Wolfram, Freidank, Neidhart,
Ulrich von Lichtenstein, Reinmar von Zweter, Tann-
häuser, Der wilde Alexander, Oswald von Wolkenstein).

13 BLOCK, Haskell M., and Robert G. Shedd. *Masters of
modern drama.* New York: Random House, 1962.

(Includes: Hauptmann, The weavers; Hofmannsthal,
Death and the fool; Schnitzler, La ronde; Wedekind,
The marquis of Keith; Kaiser, From morn to midnight;
Brecht, Mother courage, The good woman of Setzuan;
Zuckmayer, The devil's general; Dürrenmatt, The
visit; Frisch, Biedermann).

14 BRIDGWATER, Patrick, ed. and trans. *Twentieth-
century German verse.* "With plain prose translations
of each poem." Harmondsworth, Baltimore: Penguin,
1963, pb.

(Nietzsche, Liliencron, Dehmel, Holz, George, Morgen-
stern, Stramm, Hofmannsthal, Rilke, Däubler, Lasker-
Schüler, Hesse, Schröder, K. Weiss, P. Zech, Lehmann,
Stadler, Ringelnatz, Hoddis, Loerke, Herrmann-Neisse,

3

BRIDGWATER, *Twentieth-century German verse* (cont'd)
Benn, Heym, Trakl, Schwitters, Arp, Wolfenstein,
Lichtenstein, Lotz, Klabund, Werfel, Goll, Britting,
Weinheber, Bergengruen, Schnack, Kolmar, P. Gan,
I. Molzahn, Zuckmayer, Brecht, F.G. Jünger, Lang-
gässer, Kästner, Kaschnitz, Huchel, Eich, Goes, F.B.
Steiner, Schmiele, Hagelstange, Kaleko, Holthusen,
Krolow, Celan, Schnurre, Fried, Heissenbüttel, Mei-
dinger-Geise, Bächler, Piontek, Bachmann, D. Nick,
A.A. Scholl, A. Claes, Enzensberger).

15 BROCKETT, Oscar G., and Lenyth Brockett. *Plays for
the theatre.* New York: Holt, Rinehart and Winston,
1967.

(Includes: Kaiser, From morn to midnight; Brecht,
The good woman of Setzuan).

16 BROICHER, Daisy. *German lyrics and ballads done into
English verse.* New York: Gordon Press, 1977? (1912).
(Brentano, Eichendorff, Hebbel, Hölderlin, Lenau,
Meyer, Mörike, Platen, Storm).

17 BUSCH, Marie. *Selected Austrian short stories.* New
York: Oxford, 1929; Freeport, N.Y.: Books for Libraries
Press, 1971.

(Grillparzer, Ebner-Eschenbach, Saar, Braun, Strobl,
Hohlbaum, Chiavacci, Müller-Guttenbrunn, Schnitzler,
Bahr.

18 CAPUTI, Anthony. *Masterworks of world drama.* New
York: Heath, 1968, pb.
(Includes: V: Lessing, Miss Sara Sampson; Schiller,
The death of Wallenstein; VI: Kleist, Prince Fried-
rich of Homburg; Büchner, Danton's death).

19 CERF, Bennett A., ed. *Great German short novels and stories*. New York: Modern Library, 1933.

(Goethe, The sorrows of Werther; Schiller, The sport of destiny; Hoffmann, The history of Krakatuk; Grimm, Hansel and Gretel, Cinderella; Heine, Gods in exile; Storm, Immensee; Keller, The naughty saint Vitalis; Sudermann, The New Year's Eve confession; Schnitzler, The fate of the baron; Hauptmann, Flagman Thiel; Wassermann, Lukardis; Thomas Mann, Death in Venice; Stefan Zweig, Amok; Arnold Zweig, The parcel).

20 CHASE, Geoffrey H., trans. *Poems from the German*. 2 vols. Edinburgh: Blackwood, 1959 (I) and 1961 (II).

21 CLARK, Barrett H., ed. *World drama: An anthology*. 2 vols. New York: Dover Publ., 1933, 1955, pb; London: Mayflower Books, 1956.

22 CONSTANTINE, David, ed. *German short stories/Deutsche Kurzgeschichten*. Bilingual. Harmondsworth: Penguin, 1976, pb.

23 CORRIGAN, Robert W., ed. *Masterpieces of the modern Central European theatre*. New York: Collier, 1967, pb.

(Includes: Schnitzler, Game of love, La ronde: Hofmannsthal, Electra).

24 -----, ed. *Masterpieces of the modern German theatre*. London: Macmillan, 1967, pb; New York: Collier, 1967, pb.

(Büchner, Woyzeck; Hebbel, Maria Magdalena; Hauptmann, The weavers; Wedekind, The marquis of Keith; Brecht, The Caucasian chalk circle).

5

25 CORRIGAN, Robert W., ed. *The modern theatre*. New
York: Macmillan, 1964, 1970.

(Includes: Büchner, Woyzeck; Hebbel, Maria Magda-
lena; Hauptmann, The weavers; Schnitzler, La ronde;
Wedekind, The marquis of Keith; Hofmannsthal,
Electra; Brecht, The Caucasian chalk circle; Frisch,
The Chinese wall; Dürrenmatt, The visit).

26 -----, and Martin Esslin. *The new theatre of Europe*.
4 vols. New York: Dell, 1962-70, pb.

(Includes: II: Brecht, Mother Courage; Grass, The
wicked cooks; III: Dorst, The curve; IV: Hochwälder,
The raspberry picker; Handke, Self-accusation).

27 CREEKMORE, Hubert. *Lyrics of the middle ages*. New
York: Grove, 1959.

(Anonymous, Dietmar, Friedrich von Hausen, Hartmann,
Morungen, Kürenberg, Neidhart, Reinmar von Hagenau,
Reinmar von Zweter, Walther, Wolfram).

28 DEICKE, Günther, ed. *Time for dreams: Poetry from the
German Democratic Republic*. Trans. Jack Mitchell.
Berlin, Seven Seas, 1976.

(Johannes Bobrowski, Hanns Cibulka, Jo Schulz, Wal-
ter Werner, Franz Fühmann, Paul Wiens, Günther Deicke,
Helmut Preissler, Uwe Berger, Jens Gerlach, Armin
Müller, Günter Kunert, Eva Strittmatter, Adolf
Endler, Heinz Kahlau, Manfred Streubel, Wolfgang
Tilgner, Uwe Gressmann, Reiner Kunze, Wolf Kirsten,
Rainer Kirsch, Sarah Kirsch, Karl Mickel, Heinz
Czechowski, Jochen Laabs, Peter Gosse, Volker Braun,
Bernd Jentzsch, Harald Gerlach, Gerd Eggers).

29 DEUTSCH, Babette. *Contemporary German poetry*. Trans.
Babette Deutsch and Avrahm Yarmolinsky. Freeport,
N.Y.: Books for Libraries Press, 1969 (1923).
(Liliencron, Holz, Dehmel, Dauthendey, George,
Rilke, Mombert, Morgenstern, Lasker-Schüler, Wer-
fel, Hatzfeld, Brod, Goll, Ehrenstein, Klemm, Trakl,
Wegner, Klabund, Benn, Heym, Zech, Leonhardt, Hey-
nicke, Becher, Paul Mayer, Vagts, Stadler, Schickele,
Hermann-Neisse, Claire Studer-Goll, Däubler, Lich-
tenstein).

30 ENGEL, E.J., ed. *German narrative prose: Volume I*.
London: Wolff, 1965 (Vol. II: see W.E. Yuill).
(Kleist, Saint Cecilia; Arnim, The madman of Fort
Ratonneau; Tieck, Life's superfluence; Stifter,
Abdias; Grillparzer, The poor musician; Keller,
The flag of the company of seven; Storm, The
senator's sons; Holz and Schlaf, A death).

31 ESSLIN, Martin, ed. *The genius of the German theater*.
New York: New American Library/Mentor, 1968, pb.
(Lessing, Emilia Galotti; Goethe, Faust I; Schiller,
Death of Wallenstein; Kleist, Prince Frederick of
Homburg; Büchner, Leonce and Lena; Wedekind, King
Nicolo; Brecht, The Caucasian chalk circle).

32 -----, ed. *Three German plays*. Harmondsworth:
Penguin, 1963, pb.
(Büchner, Woyzeck; Hauptmann, Before dawn; Brecht:
The threepenny opera).

33 FLORES, Angel, ed. *Anthology of German poetry from
Hölderlin to Rilke*. Bilingual. London: Mayflower
Books; New York: Doubleday, 1960, pb; Gloucester,

FLORES, *Anthology of German poetry from Hölderlin to Rilke* (cont'd).

Mass.: P. Smith, 1965.

(Brentano, Droste-Hülshoff, Eichendorff, George, Heine, Hölderlin, Hofmannsthal, Lenau, Mörike, Morgenstern, Novalis, Platen, Rilke, Trakl).

34 -----, ed. *Nineteenth century German tales.* New York: Doubleday, 1959; New York: Ungar, 1966, pb.

(Gotthelf, The black spider; Hoffmann, The mines at Falun; Keller, Meret; Kleist, Michael Kohlhaas; Mörike, Mozart on his way to Prague; Jean Paul, Life of the cheerful schoolmaster; Stifter, Brigitta).

35 FORSTER, Leonard, ed. *The Penguin book of German verse.* "With plain prose translations of each poem." Harmondsworth, Baltimore: Penguin, 1957, 1961, pb.

Hildebrandslied, Muspilli, Weingartner Reisesegen, Kürenberg, Dietmar, Veldeke, Friedrich von Hausen, Morungen, Reinmar, Walther, Wolfram, Neidhart, Steinmar, Der wilde Alexander, Der guotaere, Der mîsnaere, Tauler, Ballads, Luther, Zwingli, Hutten, Johann Hesse, Anonymous lyrics 1400-1700, Weckherlin, Rickart, Spee, Opitz, Logau, Dach, Rist, Gerhardt, Fleming, Gryphius, Klaj, Hofmannswaldau, Angelus Silesius, Grimmelshausen, Stieler, Knorr, Kuhlmann, Günther, Gellert, Klopstock, Claudius, Bürger, Hölty, Goethe, Müller, Lenz, Tiedge, Schiller, Hebel, Hölderlin, Novalis, Brentano, Uhland, Eichendorff, Rückert, Platen, Droste-Hülshoff, Heine, Lenau, Zuccalmaglio, Mörike, Storm, Groth, Keller, Meyer, Nietzsche, Holz, Dehmel, George, Morgenstern, Stramm, Hofmannsthal, Rilke, Carossa, Schröder,

FORSTER, *The Penguin book of German verse* (cont'd).
Lehmann, Stadler, Loerke, Benn, Trakl, Heym,
Werfel, Brecht, Langgässer, Zuckmayer, F.G. Jünger).

36 FRANCKE, Kuno, and W.G. Howard, eds. *The German
classics of the nineteenth and twentieth centuries.*
New York: AMS Press, 1969, 20 vols.
(I, II: Goethe; III: Schiller; IV: Jean Paul,
Wilhelm von Humboldt, A.W. Schlegel, Friedrich
Schlegel, Novalis, Hölderlin, Tieck, Kleist; V:
Schleiermacher, Fichte, Schelling, Arnim, Brentano,
J. Grimm, W. Grimm, Arndt, Körner, Schenkendorf,
Uhland, Eichendorff, Chamisso, Hoffmann, Fouqué,
Hauff, Rückert, Platen; VI: Heine, Grillparzer,
Beethoven; VII: Hegel, Bettina von Arnim, Immermann,
Gutzkow, Grün, Lenau, Mörike, Droste-Hülshoff,
Freiligrath, Strachwitz, Geibel, Herwegh; VIII:
Auerbach, Gotthelf, Reuter, Stifter, Riehl; IX:
Hebbel, Otto Ludwig; X: Bismarck, Moltke, Lassalle;
XI: Spielhagen, Storm, Raabe; XII: Freytag, Fontane;
XIII: Heyse, Scheffel, Ebner-Eschenbach, Seidel;
XIV: Keller, Meyer, Widmann, Spitteler; XV: Schopen-
hauer, Wagner, Nietzsche, Emperor Wilhelm II; XVI:
Wilbrandt, Anzengruber, Rosegger, Schönherr; XVII:
Wildenbruch, Sudermann, Frenssen, Polenz, Fulda,
Hofmannsthal; XVIII: Hauptmann, Liliencron, Dehmel,
George, Rilke, Hesse, Huch; XIX: Böhlau, Viebig,
Keyserling, Thomas Mann, Thoma, Bartsch, Strauss,
Hesse, Zahn, Schaffner; XX Wassermann, Kellermann,
Halbe, Hofmannsthal, Schnitzler, Wedekind, Hardt).

37 GASSNER, John, ed. *A treasury of the theatre.* 2 vols.
New York: Simon and Schuster, 1935, 1967.

GASSNER, *A treasury of the theatre* (cont'd)
(Includes: I: Hrotsvitha, Paphnutius; Goethe, Faust
I; Schiller, Mary Stuart; Büchner, Danton's death;
Hebbel, Maria Magdalena; II: Hauptmann, The weavers,
Wedekind, The tenor; Brecht, The private life of
the master race).

38 -----, ed. *Twenty best European plays on the
American stage.* New York: Hill and Wang, 1957:
Crown, 1959.
(Includes: Kaiser, From morn to midnight; Werfel,
Jacobowsky and the colonel; Stefan Zweig, Volpone).

39 GODE, Alexander, and Frederick Ungar, eds. *Anthology
of German poetry through the 19th century.* Bilingual.
Various translators. New York: Ungar, 1964, 1972.
(Kürenberg, Morungen, Walther, Albert, Rist, Ger-
hardt, Fleming, Gryphius, Hofmannswaldau, Zesen,
Greiffenberg, Haugwitz, Hunold, Günther, Claudius,
Herder, Bürger, Hölty, Goeckingk, Goethe, Schiller,
Hölderlin, Novalis, Brentano, Kerner, Uhland,
Eichendorff, Müller, Droste-Hülshoff, Heine, Hauff,
Lenau, Mosen, Mörike, Hebbel, Herwegh, Storm,
Keller, Meyer, Leuthold, Hamerling, Busch, Saar,
Greif, Christian Wagner, Nietzsche, Liliencron).

40 HAMBURGER, Michael, ed. *East German poetry: An
anthology.* Trans. various. Oxford: Carcanet Press,
1972, pb; New York: Dutton, 1973. Bilingual.
(Brecht, Peter Huchel, Bobrowski, Günter Kunert,
Heinz Kahlau, Reiner Kunze, Sarah Kirsch, Karl
Mickel, Wolf Biermann, Kurt Bartsch, Volker Braun,
Bernd Jentzsch).

41 HAMBURGER, Michael. *German poetry 1910-1975: An anthology.* Bilingual. New York: Urizen Books, 1976, pb; Manchester, Carcanet New Press, 1977, pb.
(Lasker-Schüler, Morgenstern, Stramm, Rilke, R. Walser, E. Saenger, Lehmann, Ringelnatz, Stadler, Loerke, Benn, Trakl, Hoddis, Schwitters, Arp, Heym, Lichtenstein, Werfel, Becher, Goll, Sachs, Kolmar, Brecht, Kästner, Huchel, Kaschnitz, Jesse Thoor, Weyrauch, Walter Bauer, Eich, Franz Baermann Steiner, E. Meister, Hagelstange, Domin, Max Hölzer, Krolow, Lavant, Christine Busta, H.W. Cohn, R. Brambach, Bobrowski, M. Guttenbrunner, Schnurre, Celan, Aichinger, Heissenbüttel, Artmann, Fried, K. Raeber, Höllerer, Mayröcker, Gomringer, E. Borchers, Jandl, C. Reinig, Piontek, Bachmann, F. Wurm, K. Demus, Grass, G.B. Fuchs, Cyrus Atabay, Wieland Schmied, Enzensberger, W.H. Fritz, Kunert, Bienek, Okopenko, Rühm, Jörg Steiner, H.J. Heise, A. Endler, M.P. Hein, Th. Bernhard, K. Bayer, J. Becker, H. Hartung, Kunze, W. Kirsten, Yaak Karsunke, K. Mickel, S. Kirsch, C. Meckel, H. Czechowski, Biermann, K. Bartsch, N. Born, K. Lorenc, U. Braun, R.D. Brinkmann, B. Jentzsch, G. Vesper, P. Handke, F.C. Delius, J. Theobaldy).

42 -----, and Christopher Middleton, eds. *Modern German poetry, 1910-1960.* Bilingual. London: MacGibbon and Kee, 1962, 1966; New York: Grove Press, 1964, pb.
(Lasker-Schüler, Wolfskehl, Morgenstern, Stramm, Rilke, Däubler, Lehmann, Ringelnatz, Stadler, Hoddis, Loerke, Ball, Benn, Herrmann-Neisse, Ehren-Stein, Trakl, Arp, Heym, Lichtenstein, Werfel,

HAMBURGER, Michael, and Christopher Middleton, eds.
Modern German poetry, 1910-1960 (cont'd).

 Klabund, Becher, Goll, Schnack, Kolmar, Zollinger,
Brecht, Kästner, Huchel, Walter Bauer, Thoor, Zemp,
Weyrauch, Eich, J.B. Steiner, Hagelstange, Holt-
husen, Krolow, Lavant, Busta, Cohn, Brambach,
Schnurre, Celan, Heissenbüttel, Artmann, Fried,
Höllerer, Piontek, Scholl, Bachmann, Grass, Enzens-
berger, Schmied, Okopenko, Meckel).

43 HATCHER, Harlan. *Modern continental dramas.* New
York: Harcourt Brace, 1941.

 (Includes: Hauptmann, Hannele; Toller, Transfiguration).

44 KAUFMANN, Walter, ed. and trans. *Twenty-five German
poets: A bilingual collection.* New York: Norton,
1975, pb. Originally published as *Twenty German
poets* (New York: Random, 1962).

 (Angelus Silesius, Klopstock, Claudius, Goethe,
Schiller, Hölderlin, Novalis, Eichendorff, Uhland,
Heine, Meyer, Dahn, Nietzsche, George, Hofmannsthal,
Morgenstern, Rilke, Trakl, Werfel, Benn, Klabund,
Kästner, Hesse, Brecht, Böll).

45 KESTEN, Hermann, ed. *The blue flower.* New York:
Roy, 1946.

 (Arnim, The mad veteran of the fort Ratonneau;
Brentano, Loreley and Marmot; Goethe, The new
Melusina; Grillparzer, The poor fiddler, Grimm,
The story of the youth who went forth to learn what
fear was; Heine, Florentine nights--Second night;
Hoffmann, The Cremona violin; Keller, Spiegel, the

KESTEN, *The blue flower* (cont'd).

kitten; Kleist, The earthquake in Chile; Schiller,
The sport of destiny; Tieck, Auburn Egbert).

46 KREYMBORG, Alfred. *Poetic drama.* New York: Modern
Age, 1941.

(Includes: Hans Sachs, The wandering scholar from
Paradise; Goethe, Tasso; Schiller, The death of
Wallenstein; Hauptmann, The white saviour).

47 LAMPORT, F.J., ed. and trans. *Five German tragedies.*
Harmondsworth: Penguin, 1969, pb.

(Lessing, Emilia Galotti; Goethe, Egmont; Schiller,
Mary Stuart; Kleist, Penthesilea; Grillparzer,
Medea).

48 ————, ed. *The Penguin book of German short stories.*
Harmondsworth, Baltimore: Penguin, 1974, 1975, pb.

(Goethe, Hoffmann, Kleist, Büchner, Storm, Keller,
Heyse, Hauptmann, Schnitzler, Thomas Mann, Kafka,
Gaiser, Böll).

49 LANGE, Victor, ed. *Great German short novels and
stories.* New York: Modern Library, 1952, pb.

(Brentano, The story of just Caspar and fair Annie;
Droste-Hülshoff, The Jew's beech tree; Goethe, The
sorrows of young Werther; Hauptmann, Flagman Thiel,
Heine, Gods in exile; Hoffmann, The Cremona violin;
Kafka, A country doctor; Keller, The naughty Saint
Vitalis; Kleist, The earthquake in Chile; H. Mann,
Three minute novel; T. Mann, Death in Venice; C.F.
Meyer, Plautus in the convent; Rilke, How old Timo-
fei died singing; Schiller, The sport of destiny;
Schnitzler, A farewell; Storm, Immensee; Wedekind,
The burning of Egliswyl).

50 LUSTIG, Theodore H., trans. *Classical German drama.*
New York: Bantam Books, 1963, pb.
  (Lessing, Nathan; Goethe, Egmont; Schiller, Mary
  Stuart; Kleist, Prince of Homburg; Büchner, Danton's
  death).

51 MacINNES, Isabel, trans. *A collection of German verse
in translation.* Vancouver, B.C.: n.p., 1961.
  (Chamisso, Claudius, Dehmel, Eichendorff, Folk-
  songs, Geibel, George, Goethe, Hausmann, Hebbel,
  Heine, Hesse, Hölderlin, Huch, Keller, Klopstock,
  Lenau, Liliencron, Luther, Meyer, Miegel, Mörike,
  Mueller, Münchhausen, Platen, Reinick, Rilke,
  Rückert, Schiller, Storm, Uhland).

52 MATHIEU, Gustave, ed. *German poetry: A selection
from Walther von der Vogelweide to Bertolt Brecht.*
Bilingual. New York: Dover Publications; London:
Constable, 1971, pb.

53 MIDDLETON, Christopher, ed. *German writing today.*
Trans. various. Harmondsworth, Baltimore: Penguin,
1967, pb.
  (Hans Arp, Peter Weiss, Huchel, Grass, Meckel, Wey-
  rauch, Eich, Bieler, Celan, Bachmann, Lettau, Krolow,
  Reinig, Bobrowski, Piontek, Hagelstange, Domin,
  Höllerer, Fuchs, Arno Schmidt, Fried, Konrad Bayer,
  Max Hölzer, Lind, Artmann, Kuno Raeber, Schnurre,
  Hans Bender, Reiner M. Gerhardt, Gomringer, Heissen-
  büttel, Martin Walser, Jandl, Mon, Siegfried Lenz,
  Nelly Sachs, Kunert, Nossack, Johnson, Enzensberger,
  Klaus Roehler).

54 MORNIN, Edward, ed. *Three eerie tales from 19th*
   century German. New York: Ungar, 1975, pb.
   (Gotthelf, The black spider; Droste-Hülshoff,
   The Jews' beech tree; Storm, The rider on the
   white horse).

55 MOSES, Montrose J. *Dramas of modernism.* Boston:
   Heath, 1931, 1941.
   (Includes: Kaiser, From morn to midnight; Toller,
   The machine-wreckers).

56 NEWNHAM, Richard, ed. *German short stories.* Bilingual. Harmondsworth, Baltimore: Penguin Books, 1964,
   pb.
   (Böll, Aichinger, Bender, Fussenegger, Gaiser,
   Schnurre, Lettau, Borchert).

57 NICHOLSON, Frank C., trans. *Old German love songs.*
   London: Unwin, 1907
   (Includes selections from : Dietmar, Friedrich von
   Hausen, Hartmann, Morungen, Veldeke, Kürenberg,
   Neidhart, Reinmar von Hagenau, Reinmar von Zweter,
   Spervogel, Tannhäuser, Ulrich von Lichtenstein,
   Walther, Wolfram).

58 OSERS, Ewald, trans. *Contemporary German poetry.*
   New York: Oleander Press, 1976, pb.

59 PICARD, Barbara Leonie. *German hero-sagas and folk*
   tales. Retold by B.L. Picard. New York: Walck,
   1958; London: Oxford University Press, 1958.

60 PICK, Robert, ed. *German stories and tales.* New
   York: Knopf, 1954; New York: Pocket Books, 1955, pb.
   New York: Washington Square Press, 1962, 1971, pb.
   (Brentano, The picnic of Mores the cat; Broch,

PICK, *German stories and tales* (cont'd).

Zerline, the old servant girl; Ebner-Eschenbach,
Krambambuli; Hebel, The hussar, Kannitverstan,
Unexpected reunion; Heimann, The message that
failed; Hesse, Youth beautiful youth; Hofmannsthal,
Episode in the life of the Marshal de Bassompierre;
Kafka, The metamorphosis; Keller, A little legend
of the dance; Kesten, The friend in the closet;
Lernet-Holenia, Mona Lisa; T. Mann, Death in Venice;
Schnitzler, The bachelor's death; Stifter, Rock
crystal; Wassermann, Lukardis; Ernst Weiss, Cardiac
suture).

61 PIERCE, Frederick E., and Carl F. Schreiber. *Fiction
and fantasy of German romance.* New York, 1927.

(Arnim, Eichendorff, Hölderlin, Kleist, Tieck,
Wackenroder).

62 PLOTZ, Helen. *Poems from the German.* Bilingual.
New York: Crowell, 1967.

63 Richey, M.F. *Essays on medieval German poetry, with
translations in English verse.* New York: Barnes and
Noble; Oxford: Blackwell, 1969 (Original title, 1943:
Essays on the mediaeval German love lyric).

(Kürenberg, Dietmar, Friedrich von Hausen, Veldeke,
Morungen, Albrecht von Johansdorf, Reinmar, Walther,
Wolfram, Hartwig von Raute, Neidhart).

64 -----, ed. and trans. *Medieval German lyrics.*
Edinburgh: Oliver and Boyd, 1958.

(Kürenberg, Dietmar von Aist, Friedrich von Hausen,
Heinrich von Veldeke, Albrecht von Johansdorf,
Morungen, Reinmar, Hartmann, Wolfram, Gottfried,
Walther, Neidhart).

65 RITCHIE, J.M., and H.F. Garten, trans. *Seven expressionist plays: Kokoschka to Brecht*. London: Calder and Boyars, 1968.

(Oscar Kokoschka, Murderer hope of womenkind; August Stramm, Awakening; Franz Kafka, The Guardian of the tomb; Georg Kaiser, The protagonist; Ivan Goll, Methusalem; Alfred Brust, The wolves; Ernst Barlach, Squire Blue Boll).

66 -----, ed. and trans., and J.D. Stowell, trans. *Vision and aftermath: Four expressionist wave plays*. London: Calder and Boyars, 1969.

(Carl Hauptmann, War: A Te Deum; Reinhard Goering, Naval encounter; Walter Hasenclever, Antigone; Ernst Toller, Hinkemann).

67 ROBERTS, Helen Kurz, ed. *A treasury of German ballads*. Bilingual. Trans. Helen Kurz Roberts and others. New York: Ungar, 1964.

(Bürger, Goethe, Schiller, Chamisso, Uhland, Rückert, Platen, Heine, Kopisch, Lenau, Mörike, Keller, Fontane, Meyer).

68 ROLOFF, Michael, ed. *The contemporary German theater*. New York: Avon, 1972, pb.

(Frisch, Now they sing again; Handke, The ride across Lake Constance; Sperr, Hunting scenes from Lower Bavaria; Walser, Home front; Weiss, How Mr. Mockinpott was cured of his suffering).

69 ROTHENBERG, Jerome, trans. *New young German poets*. San Francisco: City Lights, 1959.

(Bachmann, Bremer, Celan, Dreyer, Enzensberger, Grass, Heissenbüttel, Höllerer, Krolow, Piontek).

70 RUS, Vladimir, ed. *Selections from German poetry.*
Bilingual. Irvington-on-Hudson, N.Y.: Harvey House,
1966.

71 SALINGER, Herman, ed. and trans. *Twentieth-century
German verse.* Bilingual. Princeton, N.J.: Princeton
University Press; London: Oxford University Press,
1952; Freeport, N.Y.: Books for Libraries Press, 1968.
(Barthel, Becher, Binding, Carossa, Claudius,
George, Haushofer, Hesse, Hofmannsthal, Holthusen,
Huch, Kurz, Lersch, Miegel, Morgenstern, Rilke,
Seidel, Trakl, Weinheber, Werfel, Wiechert).

72 SCHER, Helene, ed. and trans. *Four romantic tales
from 19th century German.* New York: Ungar, 1975, pb.
(Tieck, Blond Eckbert; Brentano, The story of honest
Caspar and fair Annie; Arnim, the mad invalid of
Fort Ratonneau; Hoffmann, My cousin's corner window).

73 SCHOOLFIELD, George C., ed. *The German lyric of the
Baroque in English translation.* Bilingual. Chapel
Hill, N.C.: University of North Carolina Press, 1961.
(Abraham a Santa Clara, Hans Assmann von Abschatz.
Heinrich Albert, Johann Georg Albini, Anton Ulrich,
Gottfried Arnold, August Augspurger, Johann von
Besser, Sigmund von Birken, Brockes, Czepko, Dach,
C. Eltester, Gottfried Finkelthaus, Paul Fleming,
Johann Franck, Paul Gerhardt, Georg Greflinger,
Catharina Regina von Greiffenberg, Grimmelshausen,
Johann Grob, Gryphius, Christian Gryphius, Günther,
Johann Christian Hallmann, Martin Haake, Harsdörffer,
Haugwitz, Heermann, Theobald, Höck, Hofmannswaldau,
Homburg, Hudemann, Hunold, Kirchner, Klaj, Knorr von
Rosenroth, König, Kuhlmann, Laurentius von Schnüffis,

SCHOOLFIELD, *The German lyric of the Baroque in English transation* (cont'd).

G.W. Leibniz, List, Löwenstern, Logau, Lohenstein, Ludwig von Anhalt-Koethen, Melissus, Moscherosch, Mühlpfort, Neander, Neukirch, Neumarck, Omeis, Opitz, Oppelt, Plavius, Richey, Rinckhart, Rist, Roberthin, Romplet, Scheffler, Scherffer, Schirmer, Schneuber, Schoch, Schottel, Schwabe, Schwarz, Schwieger, Scultetus, Sieber, Simler, Spee, Stegmann, Stieler, Stockmann, Stolle, Titz, Tscherning, Weckherlin, Weise, Wernicke, Zesen, Zigler, Zincgref).

74 SCHWEBELL, Gertrude C., ed. *Contemporary German poetry: An anthology.* Bilingual. Introd, Victor Lange. Norfolk, Conn.: New Directions, 1964.

(Arp, Bachmann, Oliver Behnssen, Hans Bender, Benn, Thomas Bernhard, Bienek, Bobrowski, Rainer Brambach, Brecht, Christine Busta, Celan, Domin, Eich, Enzensberger, Alfred Gong, Grass, Wolfgang Hadecke, Hagelstange, Heissenbüttel, Hans Rudolf Hilty, Höllerer, Holthusen, Huchel, Peter Jokostra, F.G. Jünger, Kaschnitz, Krolow, Lavant, Lehmann, Hans Leip, Meckel, Miegel, Neumann, Piontek, Kuno Raeber, Sachs, Margot Schaupenberg, R.A. Schröder).

75 -----. *Where magic reigns: German fairy tales since Grimm.* New York: Day, 1957.

76 SEAGRAVE, Barbara G., and J.W. Thomas. *The songs of the minnesingers.* Urbana: University of Illinois Press, 1966.

(Representative selection. Musical transcription and English translations).

77 SEGEL, Harold B. *The baroque poem*. Bilingual. New York: Dutton, 1974, pb.

> (Includes translations from: Czepko, Fleming, Gryphius, Angelus Silesius, Greiffenberg, Hanke, Kuhlmann, Opitz, Hofmannswaldau, Harsdörffer).

78 SIEPMANN, Harry Arthur, ed. *German poems: Verse in translation*. London: Batchworth Press; New York: British Book Centre, 1955.

79 SOKEL, Walter, ed. *Anthology of German expressionist drama*. Garden City, N.Y.: Doubleday/Anchor, 1963, pb.

> (Kokoschka, Murderer the women's hope; Sorge, The beggar; Sternheim, The strongbox; Kokoschka, Job; Hasenclever, Humanity; Kaiser, Alkibiades saved; Goll, The immortal one; Lauckner, Cry in the street; Brecht, Baal).

80 SPENDER, Stephen. *Great German short stories*. New York: Dell, 1960, pb.

> (Aichinger, The bound man; Benn, The conquest; Böll, The man with the knives; Büchner, Lenz; Gaiser, The game of murder; Heym, The autopsy; Hildesheimer, A world's end; Hofmannsthal, A tale of cavalry; Huber, The new apartment; Kafka, In the penal colony; Keller, A little legend of the dance; Kleist, The earthquake in Chile; T. Mann, Gladius dei; Nossack, The meeting in the hallway; Rilke, Gym period; Stifter, Brigitta; Robert Walser, A village tale).

81 STEINHAUER, Harry, ed. *German stories: A Bantam dual-language book*. New York: Bantam, 1961, pb.

82 STEINHAUER, Harry, ed. and trans. *Twelve German
    novellas*. Berkeley: University of California Press,
    1977, pb. Original title: *Ten German novellas*
    (Garden City, N.Y.: Doubleday, 1969).
    (Wieland, Love and friendship tested; Kleist,
    Michael Kohlhaas; Hoffmann, Mlle de Scudery;
    Chamisso, Peter Schlemihl; Keller, Clothes make
    the man; Meyer, The sufferings of a boy; Fontane,
    Stine; Thomas Mann, The buffoon; Hauptmann, The
    heretic of Soana; Schnitzler, Fräulein Else; Kafka,
    A hunger artist; Bergengruen, Ordeal by fire).

83 TAYLOR, Ronald, and Michael Hamburger. *Three German
    classics*. London: Calder and Boyars; Levittown, N.Y.:
    Transatlantic, 1966.
    (Storm, Immensee; Büchner, Lenz; Keller, A village
    Romeo and Juliet).

84 THOMAS, J.W., ed. and trans. *German verse from the
    12th to the 20th century in English translation*.
    Chapel Hill, N.C.: University of North Carolina Press,
    1963; New York: AMS Press, 1966.
    (Dietmar von Aist, Morungen, Walther, Neidhart;
    Gerhardt, Fleming, Gryphius, Scheffler, Hofmanns-
    waldau; Günther, Klopstock, Claudius, Hölty, Goethe,
    Schiller, Hölderlin, Novalis, Brentano, Uhland,
    Eichendorff, Rückert, Platen, Heine, Lenau, Mörike;
    Hebbel, Storm, Keller, Meyer, Nietzsche, Hofmanns-
    thal, Rilke).

85 -----, trans. *Medieval German lyric verse*. Chapel
    Hill, N.C.: University of North Carolina Press, 1968.
    (Includes selections from Heinrich von Morungen,
    Hartmann, Wolfram, Reinmar, Walther, Neidhart,

THOMAS, *Medieval German lyric verse* (cont'd).
Dietmar, Kürenberg, Veldeke, Friedrich von Hausen,
Rudolf von Fenis, Oswald von Wolkenstein, Ulrich
von Lichtenstein, Der wilde Alexander).

86 -----, trans. *Medieval German tales in English
translation*. Germanische Forschungsketten 4.
Lexington: APRA Press, 1975.

(Includes selections from: Herrand von Wildonie,
Stricker, Konrad von Würzburg).

87 ULANOV, Barry. *Makers of the modern theater*. New
York: McGraw-Hill, 1961.

(Includes: Hauptmann, Hannele; Toller, Hoppla!
Such is life!).

88 WAIDSON, H.M., ed. *Modern German stories*. London:
Faber and Faber, 1961.

(Aichinger, Albers, Becker, Bender, Böll, Borchert,
Dürrenmatt, Eisenreich, Gaiser, Hesse, Hildesheimer,
Huber, Lampe, Le Fort, Lenz, Lipinsky-Gottersdorf,
Risse, Schnurre, Schroers).

89 WATTS, Harriet, ed., intro., trans. *Three painter
poets: Arp, Schwitters, Klee: Selected poems*. Harmondsworth: Penguin, 1974, pb.

90 WELLWARTH, George. *German drama between the wars*.
New York: Dutton, 1972, 1974, pb.

(Kokoschka, Job; Broch, The atonement; Tucholsky
and Hasenclever, Christopher Columbus; Zuckmayer,
The captain of Köpenick; Toller, No more peace!;
Karl Kraus, The last days of mankind).

91 -----, *Themes of drama*. New York: Crowell, 1973, pb.

(Includes: Büchner, Woyzeck; Schnitzler, Round dance;

WELLWARTH, *Themes of drama* (cont'd)
Dürrenmatt, Incident at twilight; Hochwälder, The
holy experiment).

92 WINNER, Anthony. *Great European short novels,
volume I.* New York: Harper and Row, 1968, pb.
(Includes: Kleist, Michael Kohlhaas; Hoffmann,
The sandman).

93 YUILL, W.E., ed. *German narrative prose, volume II.*
London: Wolff, 1966 (Vol. I: see E.J. Engel).
(Britting, The white slave trader; Thoma, The
girl from India; H. Mann, Abdication; Penzoldt,
The treasure; Zuckmayer, Love story; Hofmannsthal,
Bassompierre; Bergengruen, Experience on an island;
Le Fort, The judgement of the sea; Edschmidt, The
humiliating room; Kafka, A fasting showman; Borchert,
The dandelion).

II Before 1700

94 ABSCHATZ, Hans Assmann von.

Selections in: Schoolfield, *The German lyric of the Baroque*.

95 ALBRECHT von JOHANSDORF.

Selections in: Richey, *Essays on medieval German poetry*; Richey, *Medieval German lyrics*.

96 ALEXANDER, Der wilde.

Selections in: Bithell, *The minnesingers*; Thomas, *Medieval German lyric verse*.

97 ANGELUS SILESIUS.

Angelus Silesius: A selection (Der cherubinische Wandersmann). Trans. P. Carus. Chicago: Open Court; London: Paul, 1909.

98 *The book of Angelus Silesius* (Der cherubinische Wandersmann: Selections. Trans. Frederick Franck. New York: Vintage Books; London: Wildwood House, 1976, pb.

99 *The cherubinic wanderer* (Der cherubinische Wandersmann). Sel. and trans. Willard R. Trask. Introd. Curt von Faber du Faur. New York: Pantheon Books, 1953.

100 Selections in: Schoolfield, *The German lyric of the Baroque*; Forster, *Penguin German verse*; Kaufmann, *Twenty-five German poets*.

101 BALLADS, folksongs, anonymous lyrics.

Selections in: Forster, *Penguin German verse*.

102 BIRKEN, Sigmund von.

Selections in: Schoolfield, *The German lyric of the Baroque*.

103 BÖHME, Jakob.

The Aurora (Morgenröte im Aufgange). Trans. John Sparrow. London: Watkins, 1960 (1656).

104 *Confessions* (selections). Ed. W. Scott Palmer. New York: Harper, 1954 (1920).

105 *Dialogues on the supersensual life* (Vom übersinnlichen Leben). Trans. William Law et.al. New York: Ungar, 1958 (1901).

106 *Mysterium Magnum* (Mysterium Magnum). Trans. J. Ellistone and J. Sparrow. London, 1954; London: Watkins, 1924.

107 *Signature of all things, and other writings* (De signatura rerum). Trans. (1651) J. Ellistone. London: Dent; New York: Dutton, 1912.

108 *Six theosophic points and other writings*. Trans. John Rollerston Earle. Ann Arbor: University of Michigan Press, 1958 (1920).

109 *Way to Christ* (Weg zu Christo). Trans. John Joseph Stoudt. New York: Harper, 1947; London: Watkins, 1953.

110 *Way to Christ, discovered and described by Jacob Behmen* (Weg zu Christo). Los Angeles: Wetzel, 1946.

111 BRANT, Sebastian.

The ship of fools (Das Narrenschiff). Trans. William Gillis, London: Folio Society, 1971.

112 BRANT (cont'd).

The ship of fools. Trans. (verse) Edwin H. Zeydel.
New York: Dover Publ., 1962 (1944); Gloucester,
Mass.: P. Smith, 1963, pb.

113 CAESARIUS von HEISTERBACH.

The dialogue on miracles (Dialogus magnus visionum
atque miraculorum). Trans. H. Scott and C. Swinton
Bland. London: Routledge, 1929.

114 CELTIS, Conradus (Konrad Pickel).

Selections. Ed. trans., and commentary Leonard
Forster. New York: Macmillan; London: Cambridge
University Press, 1948.

115 CZEPKO, Daniel von.

Selections in: Schoolfield, The German lyric of
the Baroque.

116 DACH, Simon.

Selections in: Schoolfield, The German lyric of
the Baroque.

117 DEDEKIND, Friedrich.

The schoole of slovenrie (Grobianus). Trans.
R.F., Gent. London, 1605; rpt. Berlin: Palaestra,
1904.

118 DEPOSITIO cornuti typographici: A mirthful play
performed at the confirmation of a journeyman.
Trans. William Blades. London: Bertram Rota
1962 (lim. ed.).

119 DIETMAR von AIST.

Selections in: Creekmore, Lyrics of the Middle
Ages; Bithell, The minnesingers; Richey, Medieval

DIETMAR von AIST (cont'd).

German lyrics; Nicholson, *Old German love songs*;
Thomas, *Medieval German lyric verse*; Richey, *Essays
on medieval German poetry*; Thomas, *German verse*.

120 DÜRER, Albrecht.
Literary remains of Albrecht Dürer (Tagebuch,
selected letters, and verses). Trans. W.M. Conway.
Cambridge and New York, 1889.

121 *ECBASIS cuiusdam captivi. Escape of a certain cap-
tive*. Latin and English. Trans. Edwin H. Zeydel.
Chapel Hill, N.C.: University of North Carolina
Press, 1964, pb.

122 ECKHART, Meister.
Works. 2 vols. Trans. C.de B. Evans. London:
Watkins, 1924; Naperville, Ill.: Alec R. Allenson,
I, 1956; II, 1952.

123 *Meister Eckhart: A modern translation*. Trans.
Raymond Bernard Blakney. New York: Harper, 1957.

124 *Meister Eckehart speaks: A colloquium of the
teachings of the famous German mystic*. Trans.
Elizabeth Strakosch. London: Blackfriars; New
York: Philosophical Library, 1957.

125 *Meister Eckhart: An introduction to the study of
his works*. Trans. James M. Clark. London, New
York: Nelson, 1957.

126 *Treatises and sermons*. Trans. (from Latin and
German), James M. Clark and John Vass Skinner.
New York: Harper; London: Faber, 1958

127 ECKHART, Meister (cont'd).

Sermon on beati pauperes spiritu. Trans. Raymond
Bernard Blakney. Pawlet, Vt.: Claude Fredericks,
1960.

128 EILHART von OBERGE.

Tristrant (Tristrant). Trans. and intro. J.W.
Thomas. Lincoln, Nebr.: University of Nebraska
Press, 1978.

129 EINHARD.

The life of Charlemagne (Vita Caroli). Trans.
Lewis Thorpe. In Thorpe, *Two lives of Charlemagne*
(Harmondsworth: Penguin, 1969, pb).

130 *Vita Karoli Magni: The life of Charlemagne*. Latin
and English. Ed. Evelyn Scherabon Firchow and
Edwin Zeydel. Coral Gables, Fla.: University of
Miami Press, 1972.

131 EKKEHARDUS I, Dean of St. Gall.

*Walter of Aquitaine: Materials for the study of
his legend*. Trans. F.P. Magoun Jr. and H.M. Smyser.
New London: Connecticut College, 1950.

132 ERASMUS of Rotterdam.

The praise of folly (Enkomion morias). Trans.
H.H. Hudson. New Haven: Princeton University
Press, 1941.

133 *EULENSPIEGEL*.

*The marvellous adventures and rare conceits of
Master Tyll Owlglass*. Trans. K.R.H. Mackenzie.
London, Boston, 1860; London, New York, 1923.

134 *A pleasant vintage of Till Eulenspiegel* (Ein

EULENSPIEGEL (cont'd).

kurtzweilig Lesen von Dyl Ulenspiegel). Trans.
(from the ed. of 1515) Paul Oppenheimer. Middle-
town, Conn.: Wesleyan University Press, 1972.

135 *FAUSTBUCH.*

*The historie of the damnable life and deserved
death of Doctor John Faustus.* (The 1592 translation of P.F., *Gent*). Modernized, edited and
introduced by William Rose. London: Routledge;
New York, Dutton, 1925; Notre Dame, Ind.: University of Notre Dame Press, 1963; New York: Da
Capo Press, 1969.

136 FLEMING, Paul.

Selections in: Schoolfield, *The German lyric of
the Baroque*; Segel, *The baroque poem*; Forster,
Penguin German verse; Thomas, *German verse*.

137 FREIDANK.

Selections in: Bithell, *The minnesingers.*

138 FRIEDRICH von HAUSEN.

Selections in: Creekmore, *Lyrics of the Middle
Ages*; Bithell, *The minnesingers*; Richey, *Medieval
German lyrics*; Nicholson, *Old German love songs*;
Thomas, *Medieval German lyric verse*; Richey, *Essays
on medieval German poetry.*

139 GERHARDT, Paul.

Selections in: Schoolfield, *The German lyric of
the Baroque*; Thomas, *German verse.*

140 GOTTFRIED von STRASSBURG.

Tristan, with the surviving fragments of the

GOTTFRIED von STRASSBURG (cont'd).

Tristran of Thomas. Trans. and introd. A.T. Hatto.
Harmondsworth: Penguin; Gloucester, Mass.: P. Smith,
1960, pb.

141 *Tristan and Isolde.* (Selected passages, with
connecting summaries). Trans. (verse) Edwin H.
Zeydel. Princeton, N.J.: Princeton University
Press, 1948; London: Oxford University Press, 1949.

142 Selections in: Richey, *Medieval German lyrics.*

143 GREIFFENBERG, Catharina Regina von.
Selections in: Schoolfield, *The German lyric of
the Baroque.*

144 GRIMMELSHAUSEN, H.J.C. von.
The adventures of a simpleton (Simplicius Simplicissimus). Trans. Walter Wallich. London: New
English Library, 1962; New York: Ungar, 1963, 1973,
pb.

145 *The adventurous Simplicissimus* (Simplicius Simplicissimus). Trans. A.T.S. Goodrick. London:
Heinemann, 1912. As *Simplicissimus the vagabond*
rpt. London: Routledge; New York: Dutton, 1924.
Rpt. (original title) Lincoln, Nebr.: University
of Nebraska Press, 1962, 1969, pb. Cf. 149, 150.

146 *Courage. The adventuress. The false Messiah*
(Trutz Simplex). Trans. and introd. Hans Speier.
Princeton, N.J.: Princeton University Press, 1964.

147 *Mother Courage* (Trutz Simplex). Trans. Walter
Wallich. London: Folio Society, 1965.

148 *The Runagate Courage* (Trutz Simplex). Trans. Robert

GRIMMELSHAUSEN (cont'd).

L. Heller and John C. Osborne. Lincoln, Nebr.:
University of Nebraska Press, 1965, pb.

149 *Simplicius Simplicissimus*. Trans. George Schulz-
Behrend. Indianapolis: Bobbs-Merrill, 1965.

150 *Simplicius Simplicissimus*. Trans. Hellmuth
Weissenborn and Lesley Macdonald. London: Calder,
1964.

151 GRYPHIUS, Andreas.
Selections (some thirty sonnets) in: Marvin S.
Schindler, *The sonnets of Andreas Gryphius*
(Gainesville, Fla.: University of Florida Press,
1971).

152 Selections in: Schoolfield, *The German lyric of
the Baroque*; Segel, *The baroque poem*; Forster,
Penguin German verse; Gode, *Anthology of German
poetry*; Thomas, *German verse*.

153 *GUDRUN*.
Gudrun. Trans. Margery Armour. London: Dent;
New York: Dutton (Everyman's Library), 1932.

154 GÜNTHER, Christian.
Selections in: Thomas, *German verse*.

155 HARTMANN von AUE.
Der arme Heinrich. Trans. (verse) C.H. Bell,
Peasant life in Old German epics (New York, 1931,
1965).

156 *Gregorius: A medieval Oedipus legend*. Trans.
(verse) and introd. Edwin H. Zeydel and Bayard Q.
Morgan. Chapel Hill, N.C.: University of North

HARTMANN von AUE (cont'd).

Carolina Press, 1955; New York: AMS Press, 1966.

157 *Gregorius: The good sinner.* Bilingual. Trans. (verse) Sheema Z. Buehne. Intro. H. Adolf. New York: Ungar, 1966.

158 *Selections.* Trans. (into English Verse) Margaret Richey. Dundee: Dr. M.F. Richey, 1962.

159 Selections in: Creekmore, *Lyrics of the Middle Ages*; Bithell, *The minnesingers*; Richey, *Medieval German lyrics*; Nicholson, *Old German love songs*; Thomas, *Medieval German lyric verse.*

160 HEINRICH von MORUNGEN.
Selections in: Creekmore, *Lyrics of the Middle Ages*; Bithell, *The minnesingers*; Nicholson, *Old German love songs*; Thomas, *Medieval German lyric verse*; Richey, *Essays on medieval German poetry*; Thomas, *German verse.*

161 HARTWIG von RAUTE
Selections in: Richey, *Essays on medieval German poetry.*

162 HEINRICH von VELDEKE.
Selections in: Bithell, *The minnesingers*; Richey, *Medieval German lyrics*; Nicholson, *Old German love songs*; Thomas, *Medieval German lyric verse*; Richey, *Essays on medieval German poetry.*

163 *THE HELIAND.*
The Heliand. Trans. Mariana Scott. Chapel Hill: University of North Carolina Press, 1966.

164 HERRAND von WILDONIE.

The tales and songs of Herrand von Wildonie. Ed.
and trans. into English verse by J.W. Thomas.
Lexington: University of Kentucky Press, 1972.

165 Selections in: Thomas, Medieval German tales.

166 HILDEBRANDSLIED.

"Hildebrandslied." Trans. Leonard Forster. In
Forster, Penguin German verse.

167 HOFMANNSWALDAU, Christian Hofmann von.

Selections in: Schoolfield, The German lyric of
the Baroque; Segel, The baroque poem; Forster, Penguin German verse; Thomas, German verse.

168 HROTSVITHA von GANDERSHEIM.

See: Roswitha von Gandersheim.

169 HUTTEN, Ulrich von, and others.

On the eve of the Reformation: Letters of obscure
men (Epistolae obscurorum virorum). Trans. Francis
Griffin Stokes. New York, London: Harper and Row,
1964.

170 JOHANN von HILDESHEIM.

Story of the three kings: Melchior, Balthasar,
and Jaspar. Facsimile illustrations of forty-five
woodcuts from the Strassburg edition of 1484.
Retold by Margaret B. Freeman. New York: Metro-
politan Museum, 1955.

171 JOHANNES von TEPL (Johannes von Saaz).

Death and the plowman, or The Bohemian plowman
(Der Ackermann aus Böhmen). Trans. (from the
modern German version of Alois Bernt) Ernest N.

JOHANNES von TEPL (Johannes von Saaz) (cont'd).
Kirrmann. Chapel Hill, N.C.: University of North
Carolina Press, 1958, pb.

172   *The plowman from Bohemia* (Der Ackermann aus Böhmen).
Bilingual. Trans. Alexander and Elizabeth Henderson. Introd. Reinhold Schneider. New York: Ungar,
1966, pb.

173 KNORR von ROSENROTH, Christian.
Kabbalah unveiled. Trans. S.L. MacGregor Mathers.
London: Routledge, 1951.

174 *KÖNIG ROTHER*
König Rother. Trans. and introd. Robert Lichten-
stein. Chapel Hill, N.C., University of North
Carolina Press, 1962.

175 KONRAD von WÜRZBURG.
Selections in: Thomas, *Medieval German tales*.

176 KÜRENBERG.
Selections in: Creekmore, *Lyrics of the Middle Ages*;
Bithell, *The minnesingers*; Richey, *Medieval German
lyrics*; Nicholson, *Old German love songs*; Thomas,
Medieval German lyric verse; Richey, *Essays on
medieval German poetry*.

177 LOGAU, Friedrich von.
Selections in: Schoolfield, *The German lyric of
the Baroque*.

178 LOHENSTEIN, Daniel Caspar von.
Selections in: Schoolfield, *The German lyric of
the Baroque*.

179 LUTHER, Martin.

    Luther's works. Ed. J. Pelikan and P. Lehmann.
    St. Louis: Concordia, 1955 -   , 56 vols.

180 *The works of Martin Luther.* Philadelphia, 1915–
    1932, 6 vols.

181 *Reformation writings of Luther.* Trans. B.L. Woolf.
    London: Lutterworth, 1937, 1956, 2 vols.

182 MECHTHILD von MAGDEBURG.

    The revelations of Mechthild von Magdeburg (Das
    fliessende Licht der Gottheit). Trans. Lucy
    Menzies. London: Longmans, 1953.

183 *MUSPILLI.*

    Muspilli (Extract). Trans. Leonard Forster. In
    Forster, *Penguin German verse.*

184 NEIDHART von REUENTHAL.

    The songs of Neidhart von Reuenthal. Trans. A.T.
    Hatto and R.J. Taylor. Manchester: Manchester
    University Press, 1958.

185 Selections in: Creekmore, *Lyrics of the Middle*
    Ages; Bithell, *The minnesingers*; Richey, *Medieval*
    German lyrics; Nicholson, *Old German love songs*;
    Thomas, *Medieval German lyric verse*; Richey, *Essays*
    on medieval German poetry; Thomas, *German verse.*

186 *THE NIBELUNGENLIED.*

    The Nibelungenlied. Trans. (prose) Margery Armour.
    London: Dent; New York: Dutton (Everyman's Library),
    1908, 1949.

187 *The Nibelungenlied.* Trans. (prose) A.T. Hatto.
    Harmondsworth, Baltimore: Penguin Books, 1965, pb.

188 *The Nibelungenlied*. Trans. (prose) D.G. Mowatt.
London: Dent; New York: Dutton (Everyman's Library),
1962.

189 *The Nibelungenlied*. Trans. (verse) William Nanson
Lettsom. New York: Colonial Press, 1901; Folcroft,
Pa.: Folcroft Library Editions, 1977

190 *The Nibelungenlied*. Trans. (verse) George Henry
Needler. New York: Holt, 1904.

191 *The song of the Nibelungs*. Trans. Frank G. Ryder.
Detroit: Wayne State University Press, 1962, pb.

192 NOTKER BALBULUS.
Charlemagne (De Carolo Magno). Trans. Lewis
Thorpe. In Thorpe, *Two lives of Charlemagne*
(Harmondsworth: Penguin, 1969, pb).

193 *OBERAMMERGAU Passion play.*
The Oberammergau Passion play. Trans. M.J. Moses.
New York, 1934.

194 *OBERUFER.*
Christmas plays from Oberufer. Trans. A.C. Har-
wood. London: Anthroposophical Publishing
Company, 1961; Rudolf Steiner Press, 1973, pb.

195 OPITZ, Martin.
Selections in Schoolfield, *The German lyric of
the Baroque*.

196 *OSTERSPIEL, Redentiner.*
Redentin Easter Play. Trans. A.E.Zucker. New
York: Columbia University Press, 1941; New York:
Octagon, 1967.

197 OSWALD von WOLKENSTEIN.

Selections in: Bithell, *The minnesingers*; Thomas, *Medieval German lyric verse*.

198 OTTO von FREISING.

The two cities (Historia de duabus civitatibus). Trans. C.C. Mierow. London: Oxford University Press, 1928.

199 PARACELSUS.

Selected Writings (Lebendiges Erbe). Ed. and introd. Jolande Jacobi. Trans. Norbert Guterman. New York: Pantheon, 1951, 1958.

200 REINMAR von HAGENAU.

Selections in: Creekmore, *Lyrics of the Middle Ages*; Bithell, *The minnesingers*; Richey, *Medieval German lyrics*; Nicholson, *Old German love songs*; Thomas, *Medieval German lyric verse*; Richey, *Essays on medieval German poetry*.

201 REINMAR von ZWETER.

Selections in: Creekmore, *Lyrics of the Middle Ages*; Bithell, *The minnesingers*; Nicholson, *Old German love songs*.

202 REUTER, Christian.

Schelmuffsky (Schelmuffskys Reisebeschreibung). Trans. Wayne Wonderley. Chapel Hill, N.C.: University of North Carolina Press, 1962, pb.

203 *REINKE de Vos*

A history of Reynard the fox. Trans. (1481) William Caxton. Ed. Donald B. Sands. Cambridge, Mass.: Harvard University Press, 1960

204　RIST, Johann.

Selections in: Schoolfield, *The German lyric of the Baroque*.

205　ROLLENHAGEN, Georg.

Alte newe Zeutung: A sixteenth-century collection of fables with English summaries. Ed. Eli Sobel. Berkeley: University of California Press, 1958.

206　ROSWITHA von GANDERSHAIM.

The plays of Roswitha. Trans. Christopher St. John. New York: B. Blom, 1966; New York: Cooper Square, 1966 (1923).

207　*Paphnutius.* Trans. Sr. M.M. Butler. In Gassner, *A treasury of the theatre*, I.

208　RUDOLF von FENIS.

Selections in: Thomas, *Medieval German lyric verse*.

209　*RUODLIEB.*

Ruodlieb: The earliest courtly novel. Bilingual. Trans. Edwin H. Zeydel. Chapel Hill, N.C.: University of North Carolina Press, 1959.

210　SACHS, Hans.

Raising the devil (Der farend Schüler mit dem Teufelbannen). Trans. W.H.H. Chambers. In Bates, *German drama*, I.

211　*Seven shrovetide plays.* Trans. E.N. Ouless. New York: Deane, 1930.

212　*The strolling clerk from paradise* (Der farendt Schüler im Paradeis). Trans. Philip Wayne. London: Oxford University Press, 1935.

SACHS (cont'd).

213 *Three shrovetide comedies.* Trans. B.Q. Morgan.
Palo Alto, Ca.: Stanford University Press, 1937.

214 *The wandering scholar from paradise* (Der farendt
Schüler im Paradeis). Trans. S.A. Eliot. In
Clark, *World drama*, I.

215 *The wandering scholar from paradise.* Trans. S.A.
Eliot. Im Kreymborg, *Poetic drama.*

216 *SAINT GALL Passion Play.* Trans. Larry E. West.
Medieval Classics: Texts and Studies, 6. Brook-
line, Mass.; Leiden: Classical Folia editions,
1976.

217 SCHEFFLER, Johann.
See: Angelus Silesius.

218 SPERVOGEL.
Selections in: Nicholson, *Old German love songs.*

219 STRICKER, Der.
Selections in: Thomas, *Medieval German tales.*

220 TANNHÄUSER.
*Tannhäuser: Poet and legend. With texts and
translations of his works.* Trans. J.W. Thomas.
Chapel Hill, N.C.: University of North Carolina
Press, 1974.

221 Selections in: Bithell, *The minnesingers*; Nicholson, *Old German love songs.*

222 TAULER, Johannes.
*The book of the poor in spirit, by a friend of
God* (Nachfolgung des armen Lebens Christi). Trans.
C.F. Kelley. New York: Harper, 1954.

TAULER (cont'd).

223   *Signposts to perfection* (Die Predigten). Ed. and
trans. Elizabeth Strakosch. London: Blackfriars;
St. Louis: Herder, 1958.

224 ULRICH von LICHTENSTEIN.
The service of ladies (Frauendienst). Trans. J.W.
Thomas. Chapel Hill, N.C.: University of North
Carolina Press, 1969.

225   Selections in: Bithell, *The minnesingers*; Nicholson, *Old German love songs*; Thomas, *Medieval
German lyric verse*.

226 ULRICH von ZATZIKHOVEN.
Lanzelet: A romance of Lancelot. Trans. Kenneth
G. Webster. Revised by R.S. Loomis. New York:
Columbia University Press; London: Oxford Uni-
versity Press, 1951.

227 WALAHFRID STRABO.
*Walahfrid Strabo's Visio Wettini: Text, translation
and commentary*. Trans. David A. Traill. Berne,
Frankfurt am Main: Lang, 1974.

228 WALTHER von der VOGELWEIDE.
Poems. Bilingual. Trans. Edwin H. Zeydel and
B.Q. Morgan. Ithaca, N.Y.: Thrift, 1952.

229   *Songs and sayings of Walther von der Vogelweide*.
Trans. Frank Betts. Oxford: Blackwell, 1917;
New York: AMS Press, 1977.

230   Selections in: Creekmore, *Lyrics of the Middle
Ages*; Bithell, *The minnesingers*; Richey, *Medieval
German lyrics*; Nicholson, *Old German love songs*;

WALTHER von der VOGELWEIDE (cont'd).

Thomas, *Medieval German lyric verse*; Richey, *Essays on medieval German poetry*; Forster, *Penguin German verse*; Thomas, *German verse*.

231 WECKHERLIN, Georg Rudolf.

Selections in: Schoolfield, *The German lyric of the Baroque*.

232 WERNHER der GARTENAERE.

Meier Helmbrecht. Trans. (verse) C.H. Bell in his *Peasant life in Old German epics* (New York: Columbia University Press, 1931, 1965).

233 WIRNT von GRAFENBERG.

Wigalois: The knight of fortune's wheel. Trans. J.W. Thomas. Lincoln, Neb.: University of Nebraska Press, 1977.

234 WITTENWILER, Heinrich.

Wittenwiler's Ring, and the anonymous Scots poem Colkelbie Sow: Two comic-didactic works from the fifteenth century. Trans. George Fenwick Jones. Chapel Hill, N.C.: University of North Carolina Press, 1956.

235 WIZLAW von RÜGEN.

Songs of the Minnesinger Prince Wizlaw of Rügen. Trans. John Wesley Thomas and Barbara G. Seagrave. Chapel Hill, N.C.: University of North Carolina Press, 1968.

236 WOLFRAM von ESCHENBACH.

Parzival. Trans. (prose) Helen M. Mustard and Charles E. Passage. New York: Vintage Books, 1961, pb.

WOLFRAM von ESCHENBACH (cont'd).

237   *Schionatulander and Sigune: An episode from the
      story of Parzival and the Graal.* Trans. (verse)
      Margaret F. Richey. Edinburgh: Oliver and Boyd,
      1960.

238   *The story of Parzival and the Graal* (Parzival).
      Trans. M.F. Richey. Oxford: Blackwell, 1935

239   *Parzival.* Trans. (verse) Jessie L. Weston.
      London: Nutt, 1894, 2 vols.

240   *Parzival.* Trans. Edwin H. Zeydel and Bayard Q.
      Morgan. Chapel Hill, N.C.: University of North
      Carolina Press, 1951.

240a *Parzival.* Trans. A.T. Hatto. Harmondsworth:
      Penguin, 1980, pb.

241   *Studies of Wolfram von Eschenbach with English
      verse passages from his poetry.* (Parzival,
      Willehalm, and Titurel). Trans. Margaret F.
      Richey. Edinburgh, London: Oliver, 1957.

242   *Willehalm* (Willehalm). Trans. Charles E. Passage.
      New York: Ungar, 1977, pb.

243   Selections in: Creekmore, *Lyrics of the Middle
      Ages*; Bithell, *The minnesingers*; Richey, *Medieval
      German lyrics*; Nicholson, *Old German love songs*;
      Thomas, *Medieval German lyric verse*; Richey,
      Essays on medieval German poetry.

III Eighteenth century

244 BABO, Joseph Marius von.

Dagobert, king of the Franks (Dagobert der Franken
König). Trans. B. Thompson. In Bates, *German
drama*, III.

245 BACH, Johann Sebastian.

*The Bach reader: A life of J.S. Bach in letters
and documents.* Ed. Hans David and Arthur Mendel.
1966.

246 BRÄKER, Ulrich.

*The life story and real adventures of the poor
man of Toggenburg* (Lebensgeschichte des armen
Mannes in Tockenburg). Trans. Derek Bowman.
Edinburgh: University Press, 1970.

247 BÜRGER, Gottfried August.

Lenore. Trans. Leonard Forster. In Forster,
Penguin German verse.

248 *Lenore.* Trans. Francis Owen. In Roberts,
Treasury of German ballads.

249 *Lenore.* Trans. Dante Gabriel Rossetti. London:
Ellis and Elvey, 1900; Folcroft, Pa.: Folcroft
Library Editions, 1973; Norwood, Pa.: Norwood
Editions, 1975.

BÜRGER (cont'd).

250 *Singular travels: Campaigns and adventures of
Baron Münchhausen* (Baron Münchhausens Erzählungen).
Introd. J. Carswell. New York: Dover Publ., 1960;
Gloucester, Mass.: P. Smith, 1961.

251 GOETHE, Johann Wolfgang von.
Arrangement of Entries:
1. Works, collections, selections
2. Individual works
3. Biographical, letters, miscellaneous.

252 *Five and twenty favorite Goethe poems.* Bilingual.
Trans. Wendell B. Smith. New York: Pageant Press,
1967.

253 *Goethe, the lyrist; 100 poems in new translations.*
Bilingual. Trans. E.H. Zeydel. Chapel Hill, N.C.:
University of North Carolina Press, 1955, 1959.

254 *Great writings of Goethe* (Includes Faust: Part
one, trans. Louis MacNeice). Ed. Stephen Spender.
New York, London: New American Library, 1958, pb.

255 *The permanent Goethe.* Selections. Ed. and introd.
Thomas Mann. Trans. Gustav Arlt and others. New
York: Dial Press, 1958.

256 *Poems.* Bilingual. Trans. David Luke. Gloucester,
Mass.: P. Smith, 1965.

257 *Poems of Goethe.* Bilingual. Trans. Edwin H. Zeydel.
Chapel Hill, N.C.: University of North Carolina
Press, 1957.

258 *Selected verse.* With plain prose translation of
each poem. Ed. David Luke. Harmondsworth: Penguin,
1964, 1972, pb.

GOETHE (cont'd).

259   *Three tales.* Ed. C.A. Russ. London: Oxford University Press, 1964, pb.

260   *Translations from Goethe.* Ed. G.F. Cunningham. Introd. J.V. Skinner. Edinburgh: Oliver and Boyd, 1950.

261   *Egmont.* Trans. Michael Hamburger. In Bentley, *The classic theatre.*

262   *Egmont.* Trans. F.J. Lamport. In Lamport, *Five German tragedies.*

263   *Egmont.* Trans. Theodore H. Lustig. In Lustig, *Classical German drama.*

264   *Egmont.* Trans. Anna Swanwick. In Clark, *World drama*, II.

265   *Egmont.* Trans. Willard Trask. Great Neck, N.Y.: Barron, 1960, pb.

266   *Elective affinities* (Die Wahlverwandtschaften). Trans. J.A. Froude and R.D. Boylan. New York: Ungar, 1963, pb.

267   *The elective affinities.* Trans. J.A. Froude and R.D. Boylan. In Kuno Francke, *The German classics,* II.

268   *Elective affinities.* Trans. R.J. Hollingdale. Harmondsworth, Baltimore: Penguin, 1971, pb.

269   *Elective affinities.* Trans. Elizabeth Mayer and Louise Bogan. Chicago: Regnery, 1963, pb: Westport, Conn.: Greenwood Press, 1976. Cf 315.

GOETHE (cont'd).

270   *Faust.*   Trans. John Anster.   New York: Oxford,
       1956 (1835).

271   *Faust.*   Trans. Walter Arndt.   Ed. Cyrus Hamlin.
       New York: Norton, 1976, pb.

272   *Faust.*   Trans. Barker Fairley.   Toronto: Univer-
       sity of Toronto Press, 1970, pb.

273   *Faust.*   Trans. Walter Kaufmann.   New York: Double-
       day, 1961, pb.

274   *Faust.*   Trans. A.G. Latham.   New York: Dutton,
       1951.

275   *Faust.*   Abridged.   Trans. Louis MacNeice and
       E.L. Stahl.   London: Faber and Faber, 1951, 1965;
       New York: Oxford University Press, 1954, 1961.

276   *Faust.*   Trans. Sir Theodore Martin.   Revised by
       W.H. Bruford.   New York: Dutton; London: Dent,
       1954.

277   *Faust.*   Trans. Charles E. Passage.   Indianapolis,
       Ind.: Bobbs-Merrill, 1965, pb.

278   *Faust.*   Trans. G.M. Priest.   London: Encyclo-
       paedia Britannica, 1955; New York: Knopf, 1957.

279   *Faust.*   Trans. John Shawcross.   London: Wingate;
       New York: Daub, 1959.

280   *Faust.*   Selections.   Trans. A. Swanwick.   In
       Bates, *German drama*, II.

281   *Faust.*   Trans. Anna Swanwick.   In Kuno Francke,
       The German classics, I.

GOETHE (cont'd).

282 *Faust.* Trans. Bayard Taylor. Boston, Mass.:
     Fields, Osgood, 1870-1; London: Strahan, 1871;
     London: Euphorion Books, 1949; New York: Modern
     Library, 1950; London: Sphere, 1969, 1974, pb.

283 *Faust.* Trans. Bayard Taylor. Ed. Anthony Scenna.
     New York: Washington Square Press, 1964, pb. Cf 340.

284 *Faust: Part one.* Ed. Randall Jarrell. New York:
     Farrar, Straus, and Giroux, 1976, pb.

285 *Faust: Part one.* Trans. Bertram Jessup. London:
     P. Owen; New York: Philosophical Library, 1958.

286 *Faust: Part one.* Trans. C.F. MacIntyre. Norfolk,
     Conn.: New Directions, 1957, 1962, pb.

287 *Faust: Part one.* Trans. C.F. MacIntyre. In
     Gassner, *A treasury of the theatre*, I.

288 *Faust: Part one.* Trans. Louis MacNeice. In
     Great writings of Goethe (New York: New American
     Library, 1958), ed. Stephen Spender.

289 *Faust: Part one, with a supplement* (Includes Act
     5 of part two). Trans. Bayard Q. Morgan. New
     York: Bobbs-Merrill, 1954, 1957, pb.

290 *Faust: Part one.* Trans. John Prudhoe. Manchester:
     Manchester University Press, 1974, pb.

291 *Faust: Part one.* Trans. Alice Raphael. Ed.
     Jacques Barzun. New York: Rinehart, 1955, 1960;
     New York: Heritage, 1959.

292 *Faust: First part.* Bilingual. Trans. Peter Salm.
     New York: Bantam Books, 1962, pb.

GOETHE (cont'd).

293　*Faust: Part one.* Trans. Anna Swanwick. In Esslin, *The genius of the German theater.*

294　*Faust: Part one.* Trans. Bayard Taylor. New York: Hartsdale, 1947.

295　*Faust: Part one.* Bilingual. Trans. Bayard Taylor. Ed. and rev. Stuart Atkins. London: Macmillan; New York: Collier, 1963.

296　*Faust: Part one.* Trans. Bayard Taylor. Ed. B.Q. Morgan. New York: Crofts, 1956.

297　*Faust: Part one.* Trans. Philip Wayne. Harmondsworth, Baltimore: Penguin, 1958, 1960, pb. Cf. 321.

298　*Faust: Part two.* Trans. Bayard Q. Morgan. Indianapolis, Ind.: Bobbs-Merrill, 1964, pb.

299　*Faust: Part two.* Trans. Bayard Taylor. Ed. and rev. Stuart Atkins. London: MacMillan; New York: Collier, 1962, pb.

300　*Faust: Part two.* Trans. Philip Wayne. Harmondsworth, Baltimore: Penguin, 1959, 1962, pb.

301　*From Lake Garde to Sicily with Goethe* (Italienische Reise). Trans. John Garrett. London: Macdonald, 1960.

302　*Götz von Berlichingen* (Götz von Berlichingen). Trans. Charles E. Passage. New York: Ungar, 1965, pb. Cf. 312

303　*Hermann and Dorothea* (Hermann und Dorothea). Bilingual. Trans. Daniel Coogan. New York: Ungar, 1966, pb.

48

GOETHE (cont'd).

304   *Hermann and Dorothea.* Trans. Ellen Frothingham. In Kuno Francke, *The German classics*, I.

305   *Hermann and Dorothea.* Trans. G.F. Timpson. New York: Oxford University Press; London: Mitre Press, 1950; Great Neck, N.Y.: Barron, 1953, pb.

306   *Iphigenie in Tauris* (Iphigenie auf Tauris). Trans. Sidney E. Kaplan. Brooklyn: Barron, 1953.

307   *Iphigenia in Tauris.* Trans. Bayard Q. Morgan. Stanford, Cal.: Academic Reprints, 1954; London: Bowes and Bowes, 1955, pb.

308   *Iphigenia in Tauris.* Trans. Charles E. Passage. New York: Ungar, 1963, pb.

309   *Iphigenia in Tauris.* Trans. John Prudhoe. Manchester: Manchester University Press; New York: Barnes and Noble, 1966.

310   *Iphigenia in Tauris.* Trans. A. Swanwick. In Bates, *German drama*, II.

311   *Iphigenia in Tauris.* Trans. Anna Swanwick. In Kuno Francke, *The German classics*, I.

312   *Ironhand* (Götz von Berlichingen). Adapted by John Arden. London: Methuen, 1965. Cf. 302.

313   *The Italian journey, 1786-88* (Italienische Reise). Trans. W.H. Auden and Elizabeth Mayer. New York: Pantheon Books; London: Collins, 1962.

314   *The Italian journey, 1786-88* (Italienische Reise). New York: Schocken, 1968, pb.

GOETHE (cont'd).

315 *Kindred by choice* (Die Wahlverwandtschaften). Trans.
H.M. Waidson. London: Calder, 1960, 1966; Calcutta:
Rupa, 1962. Cf. 266-69.

316 *Literary essays.* Ed. J.E. Spingarn. Trans. various.
New York: Ungar, 1964 (1921).

317 *Literary essays.* Freeport, N.Y.: Books for Libraries Press, 1968.

318 *Das Märchen.* Trans. and analysis by Waltraud
Bartscht. Lexington: University of Kentucky Press,
1972. Cf. 320

319 *The new Melusina* (Die neue Melusine). In Kesten,
The blue flower.

320 *The parable* (Das Märchen). Trans. Alice Raphael.
New York: Harcourt, Brace and World, 1963. Cf. 318.

321 *Prologue in heaven: The introductory scene from
'Faust.'* Trans. Percy Bysshe Shelley. Melbourne:
Truesdell, 1949.

322 *Roman elegies* (Römische Elegien). Bilingual.
Trans. David Luke. London: Chatto and Windus;
New York: Barnes and Noble, Harper and Row, 1977.

323 *Roman elegies and Venetian epigrams.* Trans. L.R.
Lind. Lawrence, Kan.: Regents Press of Kansas,
1974.

324 *The soothsayings of Bakis* (Weissagungen des Bakis).
Bilingual. Ed. Harold Jantz. Baltimore: Johns
Hopkins Press, 1966.

GOETHE (cont'd).

325   *The sorrows of Werther* (Die Leiden des jungen
        Werthers). Trans. Orson Falk. In Cerf, *Great
        German short novels and stories.*

326   *The sorrows of young Werther* (Die Leiden des jungen
        Werthers). In Lange, *Great German short novels.*

327   *The sorrows of young Werther. The new Melusina.*
        Novelle. Ed. Jacques Barzun. Trans. R.D. Boylton,
        J.S. Untermeyer, Victor Lange. London, New York:
        Holt, Rinehart and Winston, 1949, pb.

328   *The sorrows of young Werther.* Trans. George
        Ticknor. Ed. F.G. Ryder. Chapel Hill, N.C.:
        F.E. Coenen, 1952.

329   *The sorrows of young Werther, and selected writings.*
        (Reflections on Werther; Goethe in Sesenheim; The
        new Melusina; The fairy tale). Trans. Catherine
        Hutter. New York: New American Library, 1962, pb.

330   *The sorrows of young Werther, and the Novella.*
        Trans. Elizabeth Mayer and Louise Bogan. Foreword
        W.H. Auden. New York: Random House, 1971; New
        York: Vintage, 1973. Cf. 333-34.

331   *Stella* (Stella). Trans. B. Thompson. In Bates,
        German drama, II.

332   *The story of Reynard the fox* (Reineke Fuchs).
        Trans. Thomas James Arnold. New York: Heritage
        Press, 1954; New York: Limited Editions Club, 1954.

333   *The sufferings of young Werther* (Die Leiden des
        jungen Werthers). Trans. Bayard Q. Morgan. Lon-
        don: Calder, 1957, 1966; New York: Ungar, 1957, pb;
        Calcutta: Rupa, 1961.

GOETHE (cont'd).

334　*The sufferings of young Werther*. Trans. Harry
Steinhauer. New York: Bantam Books, 1962, pb;
Norton, 1970, pb. Cf. 325-30

335　*The theory of colours* (Die Farbenlehre). Cambridge, Mass.: MIT Press, 1970, pb.

336　*Torquato Tasso* (Torquato Tasso). Trans. Ben Kimpel
and T.C. Duncan Eaves. Fayetteville: University
of Arkansas Press, 1956.

337　*Torquato Tasso*. Trans. Charles E. Passage. New
York: Ungar, 1966, pb.

338　*Torquato Tasso*. Trans. John Prudhoe. Manchester:
Manchester University Press, 1979, pb.

339　*Torquato Tasso*. Trans. Anna Swanwick. In Kreymborg, *Poetic drama*.

340　*The Urfaust* (Urfaust). Trans. Douglas M. Scott.
Great Neck, N.Y.: Barron, 1958, pb. Cf. 270ff.

341　*West-eastern divan/West-östlicher Divan*. Bilingual.
Trans. J. Whaley. London: Wolff, 1974.

342　*Wilhelm Meister's apprenticeship* (Wilhelm Meisters
Lehrjahre). Trans. Thomas Carlyle (1824). New
York: Limited Editions Club, 1959; Collier Books,
1962; Heritage, 1965.

343　*Wilhelm Meister's years of apprenticeship*. Trans.
H.M. Waidson. London: Calder, 1978, 2 vols.

344　*Zuleika: The book of Zuleika from the Westeastern
divan* (Das Buch Zuleika). Trans. A. Grether
Scott. New York: Stechert-Hafner, 1951.

GOETHE (cont'd).

345   *The autobiography* (Dichtung und Wahrheit). Trans.
John Oxenford. London: Bohn, 1848-49; New York:
Horizon Press, 1969; London: Sidgwick and Jackson,
1971; Chicago, London: University of Chicago Press,
2 vols, 1974, pb.

346   *Autobiography: From my own life.* Trans. R.O. Moon.
Washington, D.C.: Public Affairs Press, 1949. Cf. 357.

347   *Botanical Writings.* Trans. Bertha Mueller. Hono-
lulu: University of Hawaii, 1952.

348   *Conversations and encounters.* Trans. David Luke and
Robert Pick. Chicago: Regnery; London: Wolff, 1966.

349   *Correspondence between Goethe and Carlyle.* Bilingual. Trans. Charles Elliot Norton. New York:
Cooper Square Publications, 1970.

350   *Eckermann's conversations with Goethe* (Gespräche
mit Goethe). Trans. Gisela C. O'Brien. Sel. and
introd. Hans Kohn. New York: Ungar, 1964, pb.

351   *Eckermann's conversations with Goethe* (Gespräche
mit Goethe). Trans. John Oxenford (1850). In
Francke, *The German classics*, II.

352   *Eckermann's conversations with Goethe.* Trans.
John Oxenford. Ed. J.K. Moorhead. London: Dent,
1971; New York: Dutton, 1971 (1850). Cf. 359.

353   *Goethe, the story of a man, being the life of
Johann Wolfgang Goethe as told in his own words
and the words of his contemporaries.* Trans. Ludwig
Lewisohn. New York: Farrar, Straus, 1949.

GOETHE (cont'd).

354 *Goethe's world as seen in his letters and memoirs.*
Trans. Berthold Biermann. New York: New Directions,
1949; Freeport, N.Y.: Books for Libraries Press,
1971.

355 *Goethe's world view: Presented in his reflections
and maxims.* Bilingual. Trans. Heinz Norden.
Ed. and introd. Frederick Ungar. New York: Ungar,
1963, 1969, pb.

356 *Letters.* Trans. M. von Herzfeld and C. Melvil
Sym. Edinburgh: Edinburgh University Press; New
York: Nelson, 1957.

357 *Truth and fantasy from my life* (Dichtung und
Wahrheit). Trans. Eithne Wilkins and Ernst Kaiser.
New York: Ravin; London: Weidenfeld and Nicholson,
1950. Cf. 345-46.

358 *Wisdom and experience.* Trans. Hermann J. Weigand.
London: Routledge and Kegan Paul; New York: Pantheon, 1949; New York: Ungar, 1964.

359 *Words of Goethe, being the conversations of Johann
Wolfgang von Goethe, recorded by his friend Johann
Peter Eckermann* (Gespräche). New York: Tudor,
1949, Cf. 350-52.

360 Major selections in: Forster, *Penguin German verse*;
Gode, *Anthology of German poetry*; Roberts, *Treasury
of German ballads*; Chase, *Poems from the German*;
MacInnes, *A collection of German verse*; Thomas,
German verse; Kaufmann, *Twenty-five German poets*.

361 See also: Lamport, *German short stories.*

362 HERDER, Johann Gottfried.

God: Some conversations (Gott. Einige Gespräche).

Trans. Frederick H. Burckhardt. Indianapolis,

Ind.: Bobbs-Merrill, 1962, pb.

363 *On the origin of language* (Über den Ursprung der

Sprache). Trans. Alexander Gode. New York:

Ungar, 1966, pb.

364 *Outlines of a philosophy of the history of man*

(Ideen zur Philosophie der Geschichte der Mensch-

heit). Trans. T. Churchill (1800). New York:

Bergman, 1967; Atlantic Highlands, N.J.: Humanities

Press, 1977.

365 *Reflections on the philosophy of the history of*

mankind (Ideen zur Philosophie der Geschichte der

Menschheit). Chicago: University of Chicago Press,

1968, pb.

366 IFFLAND, August Wilhelm.

Conscience (Das Gewissen). Trans. B. Thompson

(1801). In Bates, *German drama*, II.

367 KLOPSTOCK, Friedrich.

Selections in: Thomas, *German verse*; Kaufmann,

Twenty-five German poets.

368 KOTZEBUE, August von.

Egotist and pseudo-critic. Trans. W.H.H. Chambers.

In Bates, *German drama*, II.

369 LENZ, J.M.R.

The tutor. The soldiers (Der Hofmeister. Die

Soldaten). Trans. William E. Yuill. Chicago,

London: University of Chicago Press, 1972.

370 LESSING, Gotthold Ephraim.

Emilia Galotti (Emilia Galotti). Trans. Anna Gode
von Aesch. Great Neck, N.Y.: Barron, 1959, pb.

371 Emilia Galotti. Trans. Edward Dvoretzky. New
York: Ungar, 1962, pb.

372 Emilia Galotti Trans. F.J. Lamport. In Lamport,
Five German tragedies.

373 Emilia Galotti. Trans. Charles Lee Lewes. In
Esslin, The genius of the German theater.

374 Hamburg dramaturgy (Hamburgische Dramaturgie).
Trans. Helen Zimmern. Introd. Victor Lange.
Gloucester, Mass.: Smith; New York: Dover, 1962,
pb.

375 Laocoon, an essay on the limits of painting and
poetry (Laokoon). Trans. Ellen Frothingham (1874).
New York: Noonday, 1957; Farrar, Straus, Giroux,
1961, pb.

376 Laocoon. Trans. Edward A. McCormick. Indianapolis,
Ind.: Bobbs-Merrill, 1962, pb.

377 Laocoon. Nathan the wise. Minna von Barnhelm.
Trans. William A. Steel and Anthony Dent. London:
Dent; New York: Dutton, 1930, 1967.

378 Literarische Auswahl aus den Werken von Lessing
(and others). Bilingual. Ed. and trans. R.A.
Fowkes. New York: Cortina, 1960.

379 Minna von Barnhelm (Minna von Barnhelm). Trans.
Ernest Bell. In Bates, German drama, I.

380 Minna von Barnhelm. Trans. Kenneth J. Northcott.
Chicago, London: University of Chicago Press, 1972.

LESSING (cont'd).

381 *Miss Sara Sampson* (Miss Sara Sampson). Trans.
Ernest Bell. In Caputi, *Masterworks of world
drama*, V.

382 *Miss Sara Sampson*. Trans. Ernest Bell. In Clark,
World drama, II.

383 *Nathan the wise* (Nathan der Wiese). Trans. Walter
F. Ade. Woodbury, N.Y.: Barron, 1972, pb.

384 *Nathan the wise*. Selections. Trans. Ernest Bell.
In Bates, *German drama*, I.

385 *Nathan the wise*. Trans. Theodore H. Lustig. In
Lustig, *Classical German drama*.

386 *Nathan the wise*. Trans. Bayard Q. Morgan. New
York: Ungar, 1955, 1965, pb.

387 *Nathan the wise*. Trans. G. Reinhardt. Brooklyn:
Barron, 1950, pb.

388 *Theological Writings*. Trans. and introd. Henry
Chadwick. London: Black, 1956; Stanford, Cal.:
Stanford University Press, 1957.

389 LICHTENBERG, Georg Christoph.
Aphorisms and letters. Trans. Franz Mautner and
Henry Hatfield. London: Cape, 1969.

390 *The Lichtenberg reader*. Selections. Trans. Franz
H. Mautner and Henry Hatfield. Boston, Mass.:
Beacon, 1959.

391 *Lichtenberg, a doctrine of scattered occasions,
reconstructed from his aphorisms and reflexions*.
Bilingual. Ed. J.P. Stern. Bloomington, Ind.:
Indiana University Press, 1959.

57

392 MOZART, Wolfgang Amadeus.

Letters of Mozart (Briefe). Trans. M.M. Bozman.
London: Dent, 1928, 1938.

393 SCHILLER, Friedrich.

Friedrich Schiller: An anthology for our time.
Bilingual. Ed. Frederick Ungar. Trans. Jane
Bannard Greene and others. New York: Ungar,
1959, pb.

394 *The bride of Messina. William Tell, Demetrius*
(Die Braut von Messina. Wilhelm Tell. Demetrius).
Trans. Charles E. Passage. New York: Ungar, 1962,
pb.

395 *Camp of Wallenstein* (Wallensteins Lager). Trans.
J. Churchill (1846). In Bates, *German drama*, I.

396 *The death of Wallenstein.* Trans. S.T. Coleridge
(1800). In Caputi, *Masterworks of world drama*, V.

397 *The death of Wallenstein.* Trans. S.T. Coleridge
(1800). In Esslin, *The genius of the German
theater.*

398 *The death of Wallenstein.* Trans. S.T. Coleridge
(1800). In Kuno Francke, *The German classics*, III.

399 *The death of Wallenstein.* Trans. S.T. Coleridge
(1800). In Kreymborg, *Poetic drama.* Cf. 418, 423-24.

400 *Don Carlos* (Don Carlos). Trans. James Kirkup. In
Bentley, *The classic theatre.*

401 *Don Carlos, infante of Spain* (Don Carlos). Trans.
Charles E. Passage. New York: Ungar, 1959, pb.

SCHILLER (cont'd).

402   *Intrigue and love: A bourgeois tragedy* (Kabale und Liebe). Trans. Charles E. Passage. New York: Ungar, 1971, pb.

403   *Intrigue and love.* Trans. Guenther Reinhardt. Great Neck, N.Y.: Barron, 1953.

404   *Love and intrigue* (Kabale und Liebe). Trans. Frederick Rolf. Great Neck, N.Y.: Barron, 1962, pb.

405   *The maiden of Orleans* (Die Jungfrau von Orleans). Trans. John T. Krumpelmann. Chapel Hill, N.C.: University of North Carolina Press, 1959, 1962.

406   *Mary Stuart* (Maria Stuart). Adpt. Jean Stock Goldstone and John Reich. New York: Dramatists Play Service, 1958.

407   *Mary Stuart.* Trans. F.J. Lamport. In Lamport, *Five German tragedies.*

408   *Mary Stuart.* Trans. Theodore H. Lustig. In Gassner, *A treasury of the theatre*, I.

409   *Mary Stuart.* Trans. Theodore H. Lustig. In Lustig, *Classical German drama.*

410   *Mary Stuart.* Trans. Joseph Mellish and Eric Bentley. In Bentley, *The classic theatre.*

411   *Mary Stuart. The maid of Orleans.* Trans. Charles E. Passage. New York: Ungar, 1961, pb.

412   *Mary Stuart.* Trans. Guenther Reinhardt. Great Neck, N.Y.: Barron, 1950, 1958, pb.

59

SCHILLER (cont'd).

413 *Mary Stuart.* Trans. and adapted Stephen Spender.
London: Faber and Faber, 1959, 1974, pb.

414 *Mary Stuart.* Trans. Sophie Wilkins. Great Neck,
N.Y.: Barron, 1959, pb.

415 *Naive and sentimental poetry. On the sublime.* (Über
naive und sentimentalische Dichtung. Über das Er-
habene). Trans. Julius A. Elias. New York: Ungar,
1967, pb.

416 *On the aesthetic education of man, in a series of
letters* (Über die ästhetische Erziehung des Menschen).
Trans. Reginald Snell. New Haven, Conn.: Yale University Press, 1954; New York: Ungar, 1965, pb.

417 *On the aesthetic education of man in a series of
letters.* Bilingual. Ed. and trans. Elizabeth M.
Wilkinson and Leonard A. Willoughby. Oxford:
Clarendon Press, 1967.

418 *The robbers. Wallenstein* (Die Räuber, Wallenstein).
Trans. F.J. Lamport. Harmondsworth: Penguin, 1979, pb.

419 *The sport of destiny* (Spiel des Schicksals). In
Kesten, *The blue flower.*

420 *The sport of destiny.* In Lange, *Great German short
novels.*

421 *The sport of destiny.* Trans. Marian Klopfer. In
Cerf, *Great German short novels and stories.*

422 *The Thirty Years' War* (Geschichte des dreissig-
jährigen Krieges). Trans. A.J.W. Morrison. In
Francke, *The German classics,* III.

SCHILLER (cont'd).

423   *Wallenstein* (Wallenstein). Selections. Trans.
S.T. Coleridge (1800). In Bates, *German drama*, I.

424   *Wallenstein*. Trans. Charles E. Passage. London:
P. Owen; New York: Ungar, 1958; Rev. edn. New
York: Ungar, 1960, pb. Cf. 395-99, 418.

425   *Wilhelm Tell* (Wilhelm Tell). Trans. Gilbert
Jordan. Indianapolis, Ind.: Bobbs-Merrill, 1964,
pb.

426   *William Tell*. Trans. Sidney Kaplan. Great Neck,
N.Y.: Barron, 1954, pb.

427   *Wilhelm Tell*. Trans. William F. Mainland. Chicago,
London: University of Chicago Press, 1972.

428   *Wilhelm Tell*. Trans. John Prudhoe. Manchester:
Manchester University Press; New York: Barnes
and Noble, 1970.

429   *William Tell*. Trans. Theodore Martin (1847). New
York: Heritage Press, 1952.

430   *William Tell*. Trans. Theodore Martin (1847). In
Clark, *World drama*, II.

431   *William Tell*. Trans. Theodore Martin (1847). In
Kuno Francke, *The German classics*, III.

432   *Schiller's correspondence with Goethe*. Trans. L.
Dora Schmitz. In Kuno Francke, *The German classics*,
III.

433   Major selections in: Francke, *The German classics*,
III; Forster, *Penguin German verse*; Roberts, *Treasury of German ballads*; Thomas, *German verse*; Kaufmann, *Twenty-five German poets*.

434 SEUME, Johann Gottfried.

A *stroll to Syracuse* (Spaziergang nach Syrakus). Trans. Alexander and Elizabeth Henderson. London: O. Wolff, 1964; New York: Ungar, 1965.

435 WIELAND, Christoph Martin.

Love and friendship tested (Liebe geprüft). In Steinhauer, *Twelve German novellas*.

436 *Oberon* (Oberon). Trans. John Quincy Adams. New York, 1940.

IV Nineteenth century

437 ANZENGRUBER, Ludwig.

The farmer forsworn (Der Meineidbauer). Trans. A. Busse. In Francke, The German classics, XVI.

438 ARNDT, Ernst Moritz.

Selections in: Francke, The German classics, V.

439 ARNIM, Achim von.

Isabella of Egypt (Isabella von Ägypten). Trans. C.F. Schreiber. In Pierce/Schreiber, Fiction and fantasy.

440 The mad invalid of Fort Ratonneau (Der tolle Invalide auf dem Fort Ratonneau). Trans. Helene Scher. In Scher, Four romantic tales.

441 The madman of Fort Ratonneau (Der tolle Invalide auf dem Fort Ratonneau). Trans. M.M. Yuill. In Engel, German narrative prose, I.

442 The mad veteran of the Fort Ratonneau (Der tolle Invalide auf dem Fort Ratonneau). In Kesten, The blue flower.

443 Further selections in: Francke, The German classics, V.

444 ARNIM, Bettina von.

Goethe's correspondence with a child (Goethes Briefwechsel mit einem Kinde). Trans. W.S. Murray. In Francke, The German classics, VII.

445 AUERBACH, Berthold.

 Black forest village stories (Schwarzwälder Dorf-
 geschichten). Trans. Charles Goepp. Freeport,
 N.Y.: Books for Libraries Press, 1969.

446 *Little barefoot* (Barfüssele). Trans. H.W. Dulcken.
 Rev. P.B. Thomas. In Kuno Francke, *The German
 classics*, VIII.

447 BEETHOVEN, Ludwig van.

 The letters of Beethoven. Ed. and trans. Emily
 Anderson. London: Macmillan, 1961, 3 vols.

448 *Letters: Critical edition*. Ed. A.C. Kalischer.
 Trans. J.S. Shedlock. London: Dent; New York:
 Dutton, 1909, 2 vols.

449 *Letters, journals and conversations*. Trans.
 Michael Hamburger. London: Thames, 1951; New
 York: Pantheon, 1952.

450 Selections in: Francke, *The German classics*, VI.

451 BENEDIX, Julius Roderich.

 Obstinacy (Eigensinn). Trans. W.H.H. Chambers
 (1903). In Bates, *German drama*, II.

452 BIERBAUM, Otto Julius.

 Selections in: Bithell, *Contemporary German poetry*.

453 BISMARCK, Otto von.

 Bismarck the man and the statesman (Gedanken
 und Erinnerungen). Trans. A.J. Butler and others.
 London: Smith, Elder, 1898, 2 vols.

454 Selections in: Francke, *The German classics*, X.

455 BITZIUS, Albert.
See: GOTTHELF, Jeremias.

456 BÖHLAU, Helene.
The ball of crystal (Die Kristallkugel). Trans.
A. Coleman. In Francke, *The German classics*, XIX.

457 BONAVENTURA.
*Die Nachtwachen des Bonaventura/The night watches
of Bonaventura.* Bilingual. Ed. and trans. Gerald
Gillespie. Austin, Tex.: University of Texas Press,
1971; Edinburgh: Edinburgh University Press, 1972.

458 BRAHMS, Johannes.
The Herzogenberg correspondence (Briefe). Trans.
H. Bryant. London: Murray; New York: Dutton, 1909.

459 BRENTANO, Clemens.
Schoolmaster Whackwell's wonderful sons. New York:
Random House, 1962.

460 *The story of just Caspar and fair Annie* (Geschichte
vom braven Kasperl und dem schönen Annerl). In
Lange, *Great German short novels.*

461 *The story of honest Casper and fair Annie* (Geschichte vom braven Kasperl und dem schönen Annerl).
Trans. Helene Scher. In Scher, *Four romantic
tales.*

462 *The tale of Gockel, Hinkel and Gackeliah* (Gockel,
Hinkel, Gackeleja). Trans. Doris Orgel. New York:
Random House, 1961.

463 See Also: Flores, *An anthology of German poetry*;
Kesten, *The blue flower*; Pick, *German stories and
tales*; Francke, *The German classics*, V; Broicher,
German lyrics and ballads; Thomas, *German verse.*

464 BÜCHNER, Georg.

The complete collected works. Trans. Henry J. Schmidt. New York: Avon Books, 1977, pb.

465 *Complete plays and prose.* Trans. Carl R. Mueller. New York: Hill and Wang, 1963, pb.

466 *The plays of Georg Büchner.* Trans. Geoffrey Dunlop. London: Howe; New York: Viking, 1927; New York: Ravin, 1952; London: Vision, 1952.

467 *The plays of Georg Büchner* (Danton's death; Leonce and Lena; Woyzeck). Trans. Victor Price. London: Vision Press; New York: Ravin, 1952; London: Oxford University Press, 1971, pb.

468 *Danton's death* (Dantons Tod). Trans. John Holmstrom. In Bentley, *The modern theatre*, V.

469 *Danton's death.* Trans. Theodore H. Lustig. In Lustig, *Classical German drama*.

470 *Danton's death.* Trans. and adapted James Maxwell. San Francisco: Chandler Publishing, 1961, pb; London: Methuen, 1968, pb; London: Eyre Methuen, 1979, pb.

471 *Danton's death.* Trans. Henry J. Schmidt. New York: Avon, 1971, pb.

472 *Danton's death.* Trans. Stephen Spender and Goronwy Rees. In Bentley, *From the modern repertoire*, I.

473 *Danton's death.* Trans. Stephen Spender and Goronwy Rees. In Caputi, *Masterworks of world drama*, VI.

474 *Danton's death.* Trans. Stephen Spender and Goronwy Rees. In Gassner, *A treasury of the theatre*, I.

BÜCHNER (cont'd).

475   *Lenz* (Lenz). Trans. Michael Hamburger. In Taylor,
       Three German classics.

476   *Lenz*. Trans. Goronwy Rees. In Spender, *Great
       German short stories*.

477   *Leonce and Lena* (Leonce und Lena). Trans. Eric
       Bentley. In Bentley, *From the modern repertoire*,
       III.

478   *Leonce and Lena*. Trans. Eric Bentley. In Esslin,
       The genius of the German theater.

479   *Leonce and Lena*. *Lenz*. *Woyzeck*. Trans. Michael
       Hamburger. Chicago, London: University of Chicago
       Press, 1972. Cf. 487.

480   *Woyzeck* (Woyzeck). Trans. Theodore Hoffman. In
       Bentley, *The modern theatre*, I.

481   *Woyzeck*. Trans. John Holmstrom. In Esslin, *Three
       German plays*.

482   *Woyzeck*. Trans. John MacKendrick. London: Eyre
       Methuen, 1979, pb.

483   *Woyzeck*. Trans. Carl Richard Mueller. In Corrigan,
       Masterpieces of the modern German theatre.

484   *Woyzeck*. Trans. Carl Richard Mueller. In Corrigan,
       The modern theatre.

485   *Woyzeck*. Trans. Henry J. Schmidt. New York:
       Avon, 1969, pb.

486   *Woyzeck*. Trans. G.E. Wellwarth. In Wellwarth,
       Themes of drama.

BÜCHNER, (cont'd).

487   *Woyzeck. Leonce and Lena.* Trans. Carl R. Mueller.
San Francisco: Chandler Publishing, 1962, pb.

488   See also: Lamport, *German short stories.*

489 CHAMISSO, Adalbert von.
Peter Schlemihl (Peter Schlemihls wundersame Ge-
schichte). Trans. Leopold von Loewenstein-Wertheim.
London: Calder, 1957, 1970.

490   *The strange story of Peter Schlemihl.* In Steinhauer, *Twelve German novellas.*

491   *The wonderful history of Peter Schlemihl.* Trans.
F.H. Hedge. In Kuno Francke, *The German classics,*V.

492   *The wonderful history of Peter Schlemihl.* Trans.
W. Howitt (1843). London: Rodale Books; Emmaus,
Pa.: Story Classics, 1954.

493   Further selections in: Francke, *The German classics,*
V; Roberts, *Treasury of German ballads.*

494 CLAUDIUS, Matthias.
Selections in: Gode, *Anthology of German poetry;*
Thomas, *German verse;* Kaufmann, *Twenty-five German
poets.*

495 DROSTE-HÜLSHOFF, Annette von.
The Jew's beech tree (Die Judenbuche). In Lange,
Great German short novels.

496   *The Jews' beech-tree.* Trans. E.N. Bennett. In
Bennett, *German short stories.*

497   *The Jews' beech tree.* Trans. Michael Bullock.
In Mornin, *Three eerie tales.*

DROSTE-HÜLSHOFF (cont'd).

498   *The Jew's beech.* Trans. Lionel and Doris Thomas. London: Calder, 1958, 1963.

499   *The Jew's beech-tree.* Trans. Lillie Winter. In Kuno Francke, *The German classics*, VII.

500   Further selections in: Francke, *The German classics*, VII; Flores, *Anthology of German poetry.*

501   EBNER-ESCHENBACH, Marie von.
Aphorisms. Trans. G.H. Needler. Toronto: Burns and MacEachern, 1959, pb.

502   *Aphorisms.* Trans. A.L. Wister. In Francke, *The German classics*, XIII.

503   *The district doctor* (Der Kreisphysikus). Trans. Julia Franklin. In Francke, *The German classics*, XIII.

504   *Krambambuli* (Krambambuli). Trans. A. Coleman. In Francke, *The German classics*, XIII.

505   See also: Robert Pick, *German stories and tales.*

506   EICHENDORFF, Joseph Freiherr von.
From the life of a good-for-nothing (Aus dem Leben eines Taugenichts). Trans. E.N. Bennett. In Bennett, *German short stories.*

507   *From the life of a good-for-nothing.* Trans. A.L. Wister. In Kuno Francke, *The German classics*, V.

508   *The life of a good-for-nothing* (Aus dem Leben eines Taugenichts). Trans. Michael Glenny. London: Blackie, 1966. Cf. 510-11.

EICHENDORFF (cont'd).

509   *The marble statue* (Das Marmorbild). Trans. F.E.
       Pierce. In Pierce/Schreiber, *Fiction and fantasy.*

510   *Memoirs of a good-for-nothing* (Aus dem Leben eines
       Taugenichts). Trans. Bayard Q. Morgan. New York:
       Ungar, 1955, 1960, pb.

511   *Memoirs of a good for nothing.* Trans. Ronald
       Taylor. London: Calder and Boyars; New York:
       Hillary House, 1966.

512   Selections in Flores, *An anthology of German poetry;*
       Francke, *The German classics,* V; Broicher, *German
       lyrics and ballads;* Forster, *Penguin German verse;*
       Gode, *Anthology of German poetry;* MacInnes, *A
       collection of German verse;* Thomas, *German verse;*
       Kaufmann, *Twenty-five German poets.*

513 FICHTE, Johann Gottlieb.
       Addresses to the German nation (Reden an die
       deutsche Nation). Trans. L.H. Gray. In Kuno
       Francke, *The German classics,* V.

514   *Addresses to the German nation.* Trans. R.F. Jones
       and G.H. Turnbull. New York: Harper and Row,
       1968 (1922).

515   *The destiny of man* (Die Bestimmung des Menschen:
       extracts). Trans. F.H. Hedge. In Kuno Francke,
       The German classics, V.

516   *The science of knowledge* (Die Wissenschaftslehre).
       New York: Appleton, 1969.

517   *The vocation of man* (Die Bestimmung des Menschen).
       New York: Bobbs-Merrill, 1956.

518 FONTANE, Theodor.

Beyond recall (Unwiederbringlich). Trans. Douglas Parmée. London, New York: Oxford University Press, 1964.

519 *Effi Briest* (Effi Briest). Trans. W.A. Cooper. In Kuno Francke, *The German classics*, XII.

520 *Effi Briest*. Trans. (abridged) William A. Cooper. New York: Ungar, 1966, pb.

521 *Effi Briest*. Trans. Douglas Parmée. Harmondsworth, Baltimore: Penguin, 1967, 1976, pb.

522 *Effi Briest*. Trans. Walter Wallich. London: New English Library, 1962, pb.

523 *Grete Minde* (Grete Minde). London: Methuen, 1955.

524 *Jenny Treibel* (Frau Jenny Treibel). Trans. Ulf Zimmermann. New York: Ungar, 1976, pb.

525 *A man of honor: Schach von Wuthenow*. Trans. E.M. Valk. New York: Ungar, 1975, pb.

526 *My childhood days* (Meine Kinderjahre). Trans. (extracts) W.A. Cooper. In Kuno Francke, *The German classics*, XII.

527 *Sir Ribbeck of Ribbeck of Havelland* (Herr von Ribbeck auf Ribbeck im Havellande). Trans. Elizabeth Shub. New York: MacMillan, 1969; London: Abelard Schuman, 1971.

528 *Stine* (Stine). In Steinhauer, *Twelve German novellas*.

529 *A suitable match* (Irrungen, Wirrungen). Trans. Sandra Morris. London, Glasgow: Blackie, 1968.

FONTANE (cont'd).

530   Selections in: Roberts, *Treasury of German ballads.*

531   FOUQUÉ, Friedrich de la Motte.

Undine, and other stories. Introd. Sir Edmund
Gosse. London: Oxford University Press/The World's
Classics, 1932.

532   *Undine* (Undine: Selections). Trans. F.E. Bunnett.
In Kuno Francke, *The German classics,* V.

533   *Undine.* Trans. Paul Turner. London: Calder, 1960,
1966, pb.

534   FREILIGRATH, Ferdinand.

Selections in: Francke, *The German classics,* VII.

535   FREYTAG, Gustav.

Doctor Luther (Doktor Luther). Trans. E.H. Babbitt.
In Kuno Francke, *The German classics,* XII.

536   *Frederick the Great.* Trans. E.H. Babbitt. In Kuno
Francke, *The German classics,* XII.

537   *The journalists* (Die Journalisten). Trans. E.F.
Henderson. In Kuno Francke, *The German classics,*
XII.

538   *Debit and credit* (Soll und Haben). Trans. L.C.
Cumming. New York: Abbatt, 1909 (1857).

539   FULDA, Ludwig.

Selections in: Francke, *The German classics,* XVII.

540   GEIBEL, Emanuel.

Selections in: Francke, *The German classics,* VII.

541   GOTTHELF, Jeremias.

The black spider (Die schwarze Spinne). Trans.

GOTTHELF (cont'd).

Mary Hottinger. In Flores, *Nineteenth century German tales.*

542 *The black spider.* Trans. Mary Hottinger. In Mornin, *Three eerie tales.*

543 *The black spider.* Trans. H.M. Waidson. London: Calder, 1956, 1958; New York: McClelland, 1958.

544 *Uli, the farmhand* (Uli, der Knecht). Abridged trans. B.Q. Morgan. In Kuno Francke, *The German classics,* VIII.

545 *Wealth and welfare* (Geld und Geist). London: A. Strahan, 1867; rpt. New York: Fertig, 1976.

546 GRABBE, Christian Dietrich.
Jest, satire, irony (Scherz, Satire, Ironie und tiefere Bedeutung). Trans. Maurice Edwards. In Bentley, *From the modern repertoire,* II.

547 *Jest, satire, irony, and deeper significance* (Scherz, Satire, Ironie und tiefere Bedeutung). Trans. Maurice Edwards. New York: Ungar, 1966, pb.

548 *Comedy, satire, irony and deeper meaning* (Scherz, Satire, Ironie und tiefere Bedeutung). Trans. Barbara Wright. London: Gaberbocchus Press, 1955.

549 GRILLPARZER, Franz.
Plays on classic themes (Sappho; The golden fleece; The waves of sea and love). Trans. Samuel Solomon. New York: Random House, 1969.

550 *A dream is life* (Der Traum ein Leben). Trans. Henry H. Stevens. Yarmouthport, Mass.: Register Press, 1946.

GRILLPARZER (cont'd).

551   *Family strife in Habsburg* (Bruderzwist in Habsburg).
        Trans. Arthur Burkhard. Yarmouthport, Mass.:
        Register Press, 1949.

552   *The golden fleece: The guest-friend, The Argonauts*
        (Das goldene Vliess). Trans. A. Burkhard. Yar-
        mouthport, Mass.: Register Press, 1942.

553   *Hero and Leander; The waves of sea and of love*
        (Des Meeres und der Liebe Wellen). Trans. Arthur
        Burkhard. Yarmouthport, Mass.: Register Press,
        1962.

554   *The Jewess of Toledo* (Die Jüdin von Toledo). Trans.
        G.H. and A.P. Danton. In Kuno Francke, *The German
        classics*, VI.

555   *The Jewess of Toledo. Esther.* Trans. Arthur
        Burkhard. Yarmouthport, Mass.: Register Press,
        1953.

556   *King Ottocar: His rise and fall* (König Ottokars
        Glück und Ende). Trans. Arthur Burkhard. Yar-
        mouthport, Mass.: Register Press, 1962.

557   *Libussa* (Libussa). Trans. H.H. Stevens. Yar-
        mouthport, Mass.: Register Press, 1941.

558   *Medea* (Medea). Trans. Arthur Burkhard. Yarmouth-
        port, Mass.: Register Press, 1941, 1956.

559   *Medea.* Trans. F.J. Lamport. In Lamport, *Five
        German tragedies.*

560   *Medea.* Trans. T.A. Miller. In Kuno Francke, *The
        German classics*, VI.

GRILLPARZER (cont'd).

561   *The poor fiddler* (Der arme Spielmann). In Kesten,
        The blue flower.

562   *The poor fiddler.* Trans. Alexander and Elizabeth
        Henderson. Introd. Ivar Ivask. New York: Ungar,
        1967, pb.

563   *The poor musician* (Der arme Spielmann). Trans.
        J.F. Hargreaves and J.G. Cumming. In Engel,
        German narrative prose, I.

564   *The poor musician.* Trans. Alfred Remy. In Kuno
        Francke, *The German classics*, VI.

565   *Sappho* (Sappho). Trans. Arthur Burkhard. Yar-
        mouthport, Mass.: Register Press, 1953.

566   *Thou shalt not lie* (Weh dem der lügt). Trans.
        H.H. Stevens. Yarmouthport, Mass.: Register Press,
        1939.

567 GRIMM, Jakob and Wilhelm.
        Fairy tales (Kinder- und Hausmärchen). Trans.
        Mrs. Edgar Lucas and others. New York: Grosset
        and Dunlap, 1945; New York: Parents Magazine
        Cultural Institute, 1966.

568   *Fairy tales.* Trans. E. Taylor. Harmondsworth:
        Penguin, 1971.

569   *Favourite fairy tales told in Germany* (Kinder-
        und Hausmärchen). Trans. Virginia Haviland.
        Boston: Little, Brown, 1959.

570   *Grimm's fairy tales: Complete edition* (Kinder-
        und Hausmärchen). Trans. M. Hunt and J. Stern.
        New York: Pantheon, 1944.

GRIMM, Jakob and Wilhelm (cont'd).

571   *The Grimms' German folk tales* (Kinder- und Haus-
märchen). Trans. Francis P. Magoun, Jr., and
Alexander Krappe. Carbondale, Ill.: Southern
Illinois University Press, 1960.

572   *Grimm's other tales.* A new selection by Wilhelm
Hansen. Trans. Ruth Michaelis-Jena and Arthur
Ratcliff. London: Golden Cockerel, 1956; South
Brunswick, N.J.: A.S. Barnes, 1966.

573   *Household stories from the collection of the
brothers Grimm.* Trans. Lucy Crane. New York:
MacMillan, 1949, 1954; McGraw Hill, 1966.

574   *Grimms' tales for young and old: The complete
stories* (Kinder- und Hausmärchen). Trans. Ralph
Manheim. Garden City, N.Y.: Doubleday, 1977.

575 GRÜN, Anastasius.
Selections in: Francke, *The German classics*, VII.

576 GUTZKOW, Karl Ferdinand.
Sword and queue (Zopf und Schwert). Trans. G.I.
Colbron. In Kuno Francke, *The German classics*,
VII.

577   *Wally die Zweiflerin: Wally the skeptic.* Trans.
with intro. and notes Ruth-Ellen Boetcher Joeres.
Bern, Frankfurt am Main: Lang, 1974.

578 HALBE, Max.
Mother Earth (Mutter Erde). Trans. P.H. Grummann.
In Francke, *The German classics*, XX.

579   *Youth* (Jugend). Trans. S.T. Barrows. New York:
1916.

580 HARDENBERG, Friedrich von.
     See: NOVALIS.

581 HAUFF, Wilhelm.
     Tales (Märchen). Trans. S. Mendel. Freeport,
     N.Y.: Books for Libraries Press, 1970.

582 *Fairy tales.* Trans. J. Emerson and others.
     London: Cape, 1971.

583 *Dwarf Long-Nose* (Der Zwerg Nase). Trans. Doris
     Orgel. New York: Random House, 1960; London:
     Bodley Head, 1979.

584 Selections in: Francke, *The German classics*, V.

585 HAUPTMANN, Gerhart.
     The dramatic works (all plays published up to
     1925). Ed. L. Lewisohn. Trans. various. New
     York, 1912-29, 9 vols.

586 *Five plays* (The weavers, The beaver coat, Hannele,
     Drayman Henschel, Rose Bernd). Trans. Theodore
     H. Lustig. Introd. John Gassner, New York:
     Bantam Books, 1961, pb.

587 *Before dawn* (Vor Sonnenaufgang). Trans. Richard
     Newnham. In Esslin, *Three German plays.*

587a *Before daybreak* (Vor Sonnenaufgang). Trans. Peter
     Bauland. Chapel Hill, N.C.: University of North
     Carolina Press, 1978.

588 *Flagman Thiel* (Bahnwärter Thiel). Trans. Adele
     S. Seltzer. In Cerf, *Great German short novels
     and stories.*

589 *Flagman Thiel.* In Lange, *Great German short novels.*

HAUPTMANN (cont'd).

590   *The fool in Christ, Emanuel Quint* (Der Narr in
      Christo, Emanuel Quint). Trans. T. Seltzer
      (1911). New York: Fertig, 1976.

591   *Hannele* (Hanneles Himmelfahrt). Trans. W. Archer
      (1894). In Bates, *German drama*, III.

592   *Hannele*. Trans. Horst Frenz and Miles Waggoner.
      In Ulanov, *Makers of the modern theater*.

593   *Hannele*. Trans. C.H. Meltzer. London, New York,
      1908.

594   *Hannele*. Trans. C.H. Meltzer (1908). In Hatcher,
      Modern continental dramas.

595   *The heretic of Soana* (Der Ketzer von Soana).
      Trans. Bayard Q. Morgan. New York: Ungar, 1958,
      pb; London: Calder, 1960.

596   *The heretic of Soana*. In Steinhauer, *Twelve German
      novellas*.

597   *Michael Kramer* (Michael Kramer). Trans. Ludwig
      Lewisohn. In Francke, *The German classics*, XVIII.

598   *The sunken bell* (Die versunkene Glocke). Trans.
      C.H. Meltzer. In Francke, *The German classics*,
      XVIII.

599   *The weavers* (Die Weber). Trans. Horst Frenz and
      Miles Waggoner. In Block, *Masters of modern drama*.

600   *The weavers*. Trans. Mary Morrison. In Francke,
      The German classics, XVIII.

601   *The weavers*. Trans. Mary Morrison. In Gassner,
      A treasury of the theatre, II.

HAUPTMANN (cont'd).

602   *The weavers.* Trans. Carl Richard Mueller. San
       Francisco: Chandler Publ., 1965, pb.

603   *The weavers.* Trans. Carl Richard Mueller. In
       Corrigan, *Masterpieces of the modern German
       theatre.*

604   *The weavers.* Trans. Carl Richard Mueller. In
       Corrigan, *The modern theatre.*

605   *The weavers, Hannele, The beaver coat.* Trans.
       Horst Frenz and Miles Waggoner. New York: Rine-
       hart, 1951; London, New York: Holt, Rinehart and
       Winston, 1959, pb; New York: Ungar, 1977, pb.

606   *The white saviour* (Der weisse Heiland). Trans.
       Willa and Edwin Muir. In Kreymborg, *Poetic drama.*

607   See also: Lamport, *German short stories.*

608 HEBBEL, Friedrich.
       Three plays (Judith; Herod and Mariamne; Gyges and
       his ring). Trans. Marion W. Sonnenfeld. Lewisburg:
       Bucknell University Press, 1974.

609   *Herod and Mariamne* (Herodes und Mariamne). Trans.
       P.H. Curts. Chapel Hill, N.C.: University of
       North Carolina Press, 1950.

610   *Maria Magdalena* (Maria Magdalene). Trans. Barker
       Fairley. In Gassner, *A treasury of the theatre,* I.

611   *Maria Magdalena.* Trans. Carl R. Mueller. San
       Francisco: Chandler, 1962, pb.

612   *Maria Magdalena.* Trans. Carl Richard Mueller. In
       Corrigan, *Masterpieces of the modern German theatre.*

HEBBEL (cont'd).

613   *Maria Magdalena.* Trans. Carl Richard Mueller.   In
      Corrigan, *The modern theatre.*

614   *Maria Magdalena.* Trans. P.B. Thomas.   In Kuno
      Francke, *The German classics,* IX.

615   *Recollections of my childhood.* Trans. F.H. King.
      In Kuno Francke, *The German classics,* IX.

616   *Siegfried's death* (Die Nibelungen: Extract). Trans.
      Katherine Royce.   In Kuno Francke, *The German
      classics,* IX.

617   Selections in: Francke, *The German classics,* IX;
      Broicher, *German lyrics and ballads;* Gode, *Antho-
      logy of German poetry;* Thomas, *German verse.*

618   HEBEL, Johann Peter.
      Hebel's Bible stories. Trans. Emily Anderson.
      London: Barrie and Rockliff, 1961.

619   *Francisca, and other stories.* Trans. Clavia
      Goodman and Bayard Q. Morgan.   Lexington, Ky.:
      Anvil Press, 1957.

620   Selections in: Forster, *Penguin German verse.*

621   See also: Robert Pick, *German stories and tales.*

622   HEGEL, G.W.F.
      Selections in: Francke, *The German classics,* VII.

623   HEINE, Heinrich.
      Bittersweet poems of Heinrich Heine. Trans.
      Joseph Auslander.   Mount Vernon, N.Y.: Peter
      Pauper Press, 1956, pb.

624   *Heine.* Ed. Sol Liptzin.   New York: City College
      Press, 1956.

HEINE (cont'd).

625   *Heine: Selected verse.* Trans. Peter Branscombe.
       Harmondsworth: Penguin, 1967, pb.

626   *Lyric poems and ballads.* Bilingual. Trans. Ernst
       Feise. Pittsburgh: University of Pittsburgh Press,
       1961, pb; New York, London: McGraw-Hill, 1964, pb.

627   *Poems.* Trans. and introd. Louis Untermeyer. New
       York: Limited Editions Club, 1957; New York:
       Heritage Press, 1957.

628   *Poems and ballads.* Trans. E. Lazarus. New York:
       Hartsdale, 1948; New York: Doubleday, 1950, pb.

629   *The poetry of Heinrich Heine.* Trans. Louis
       Untermeyer and others. New York: Citadel Press,
       1969, pb.

630   *The poetry and prose.* Ed. Frederic Ewen. Trans.
       Louis Untermeyer and others. New York: Citadel
       Press, 1948; 1959, pb.

631   *Prose and poetry.* Introd. Ernest Rhys. London:
       Dent; New York: Dutton, 1962.

632   *Selected lyrics.* Trans. H. Wolfe. London: Lane,
       1950.

633   *Selected poems.* Trans. Barker Fairley. Don Mills,
       Ontario: Heinrich Heine Press, 1965.

634   *Selected works.* Trans. Helen M. Mustard and Max
       Knight. New York: Vintage Books, 1973, pb.

635   *The sword and the flame: Selections from his prose.*
       Ed. Alfred Werner. Trans. C.G. Leland. New York,
       London: Yoseloff, 1960.

HEINE (cont'd).

636   *Versions and perversions of Heine.* Trans. C.H.
        Sisson. London: Gaberbocchus Press, 1955.

637   *Works: A biographical anthology.* Ed. Hugo Bieber.
        Trans. Moses Hadas. Philadelphia: Jewish Publish-
        ing Society of America, 1956.

638   *Doktor Faust: A dance poem.* Trans. B. Ashmore.
        New York: British Book Centre; London: Nevill, 1952.

639   *Florentine nights - second night* (Florentinische
        Nächte). In Kesten, *The blue flower.*

640   *Germany, a winter's tale* (Deutschland, ein Winter-
        märchen). Trans. H. Salinger. New York, 1944.

641   *Gods in exile* (Die Götter im Exil). Trans. M.
        Fleischman. In Cerf, *Great German short novels
        and stories.*

642   *Gods in exile.* In Lange, *Great German short novels.*

643   *The journey to the Harz* (Die Harzreise). Trans.
        C.G. Leland. In Kuno Francke, *The German classics,*
        VI. Cf. 650.

644   *The North Sea* (Nordsee). Bilingual. Ed. and
        trans. Howard M. Jones. LaSalle, Ill.: Open
        Court, 1973 (1916), pb.

645   *The North Sea.* Trans. V. Watkins. Norfolk, Conn.:
        New Directions, 1951; London: Faber and Faber, 1955.

646   *The Rabbi of Bacherach* (Der Rabbi von Bacharach).
        Trans. E.B. Ashton, New York: Schocken, 1947.

647   *The Rabbi of Bacharach.* Trans. C.G. Leland. In
        Kuno Francke, *The German classics,* VI.

HEINE (cont'd).

648   *Religion and philosophy in Germany: A fragment.*
Trans. John Snodgrass.   Introd. Ludwig Marcuse.
Boston: Beacon; London: Mayflower, 1959.

649   *The romantic school* (Die romantische Schule).
Trans. C.G. Leland.   In Kuno Francke, *The German
classics*, VI.

650   *The sea and the hills: The Harz journey and the
North Sea.*   Trans. Frederic T. Wood.   Boston:
Chapman and Grimes, 1946.

651   Selections in: Chase, *Poems from the German*;
Flores, *Anthology of German poetry*; Francke, *The
German classics*, VI; Forster, *Penguin German verse*;
Gode, *Anthology of German poetry*; MacInnes, *A
collection of German verse*; Thomas, *German verse*;
Kaufmann, *Twenty-five German poets.*

652 HERWEGH, Georg.
Selections in: Francke, *The German classics*, VII.

653 HEYSE, Paul.
L'Arrabiata (L'Arrabiata).   Trans. Mary Wilson.
In Francke, *The German classics*, XIII.

654   *Blind* (Die Blinden).   Trans. Mary Wilson.   In
Francke, *The German classics*, XIII.

655   *Nino and Maso* (Nino und Maso).   Trans. Alfred
Remy.   In Francke, *The German classics*, XIII.

656   *The spell of Rothenburg* (Das Glück von Rothenburg).
Trans. C.L. Townsend.   In Francke, *The German
classics*, XIII.

657   See also: Lamport, *German short stories.*

658 HÖLDERLIN, Friedrich.
   Alcaic poems. Bilingual. Trans. Elizabeth
   Henderson. New York: Ungar; London: O. Wolff,
   1962.

659 *Poems.* Bilingual. Trans. Michael Hamburger.
   London: Harvill Press, 1943, 1952; New York:
   Pantheon Books, 1953.

660 *Poems and fragments.* Bilingual. Trans. Michael
   Hamburger. London: Routledge and Kegan Paul,
   1966; Ann Arbor, Mich.: University of Michigan
   Press, 1967.

661 *Selected poems.* Bilingual. Trans. J.B. Leishman.
   London: Hogarth Press, 1944, 1954; New York:
   Grove, 1956.

662 *Selected verse.* With plain prose translation of
   each poem, introd. and notes by Michael Hamburger.
   Harmondsworth: Penguin, 1961, pb.

663 *Hyperion. Thalia fragment, 1794.* Trans. Karl
   Maurer. Winnipeg: Hölderlin Society, 1968.

664 *Hyperion* (Hyperion). Trans. W.R. Trask. New
   York, Toronto: New American Library, 1956, pb.;
   New York: Ungar, 1965.

665 *Hyperion* (extracts). Trans. C.F. Schreiber. In
   Pierce/Schreiber, *Fiction and fantasy.*

666 Selections in: Flores, *Anthology of German poetry*;
   Francke, *The German classics*, IV; Broicher, *German
   lyrics and ballads*; Forster, *Penguin German verse*;
   Gode, *Anthology of German poetry*; Thomas, *German
   verse*; Kaufmann, *Twenty-five German poets.*

HÖLDERLIN (cont'd).

667   See also: *Friedrich Hölderlin and Eduard Mörike:*
       Selected poems, trans. Christopher Middleton
       (Chicago, London: University of Chicago Press,
       1972). Bilingual.

668   HÖLTY, Ludwig.
       Selections in: Thomas, *German verse.*

669   HOFFMANN, E.T.A.
       The best tales of Hoffmann. Ed. E.F. Bleiler.
       London: Constable; New York: Dover, 1967. (The
       golden flower pot; Automata; A New Year's Eve
       adventure; Nutcracker and the King of Mice; The
       sand-man; Rath Krespel; Tobias Martin; The mines
       of Falun; Signor Formica; The king's betrothed).

670   *Four tales.* Trans. Michael Bullock. London:
       New English Library, 1962, pb. (The sandman;
       Mademoiselle de Scudery; Datura fastuosa; The
       King's bride).

671   *Eight tales.* Trans. J.M. Cohen. London: Pan
       Books, 1952, pb.

672   *Selected writings.* Trans. Leonard J. Kent and
       Elizabeth C. Knight. Chicago, London: University
       of Chicago Press, 1969, 2 vols. (I. Ritter Glück;
       The golden pot; The sandman; Councillor Krespel;
       The mines of Falun; Mademoiselle de Scuderi; The
       doubles; II. The life and opinions of Kater Murr).

673   *Tales from Hoffmann.* Ed. J.M. Cohen. New York:
       Coward-McCann; London: Lane, 1951.

674   *Tales of Hoffmann.* New York: Heritage, 1951.

HOFFMANN (cont'd).

675 *Tales of Hoffmann.* Ed. and trans. Christopher
Lazare. New York: Grove Press, 1959; London:
Calder, 1960, pb.

676 *Tales of Hoffmann.* Trans. James Kirkup. London,
Glasgow: Blackie, 1966.

677 *The tales of Hoffmann.* Trans. Michael Bullock.
New York: Ungar, 1963, pb. (The sandman; Mademoiselle de Scudery; Datura Fastuosa; The king's
bride; Gambler's luck).

678 *Three Märchen of E.T.A. Hoffmann.* Trans. Charles
E. Passage. Columbia: University of South Carolina
Press, 1971. (Little Zaches; Princess Brambilla;
Master Flea).

679 *Weird tales.* Trans. J.T. Bealby (1885). Freeport,
N.Y.: Books for Libraries Press, 1970.

680 *Coppelia* (Der Sandmann). Trans. Yvonne Sebasta-
kava. London: Dent, 1971.

681 *The Cremona violin* (Rat Krespel). In Kesten, *The
blue flower.*

682 *The Cremona violin.* In Lange, *Great German short
novels.*

683 *The devil's elixirs* (Die Elixiere des Teufels).
Trans. Ronald Taylor. London: Calder and Boyars,
1963, 1966, pb.

684 *The golden pot* (Der goldene Topf). Trans. F.H.
Hedge. In Kuno Francke, *The German classics*, V.

685 *The history of Krakatuk.* Trans. William Makepeace

HOFFMANN (cont'd).

Thackeray. In Cerf, *Great German short novels and stories.*

686 *The king's bride* (Die Königsbraut). Trans. Paul Turner. London: Calder, 1959, 1963.

687 *Mademoiselle de Scudéry* (Das Fräulein von Scuderi). In Steinhauer, *Twelve German novellas.*

688 *The mines of Falun* (Die Bergwerke zu Falun). Trans. E.N. Bennett. In Bennett, *German short stories.*

689 *The mines at Falun* (Die Bergwerke zu Falun). Trans. Peggy Sard. In Flores, *Nineteenth century German tales.*

690 *My cousin's corner window* (Des Vetters Eckfenster). Trans. Helene Scher. In Scher, *Four romantic tales.*

691 *Nutcracker and the Mouse King* (Nussknacker und Mäusekönig). Trans. M.B. Donald. Bromley: Typlan, 1972.

692 *The sandman* (Der Sandmann). Trans. Michael Bullock. In Winner, *Great European short novels*, I.

693 *Selected letters.* Trans. Johanna C. Sahlin. Chicago: University of Chicago Press, 1977.

694 See also: Lamport, *German short stories.*

695 HOLZ, Arno.
Selections in: Deutsch, *Contemporary German poetry.*

696 and Johannes Schlaf. *A death.* Trans. J.R. Davies. In Engel, *German narrative prose*, I.

697 IMMERMANN, Karl Lebrecht.

The Oberhof (Der Oberhof). Trans. P.B. Thomas.
In Kuno Francke, *The German classics*, VII.

698 JEAN PAUL.

*Horn of Oberon: Jean Paul Richter's school for
Aesthetics* (Vorschule der Ästhetik). Trans.
Margaret Hale. Detroit: Wayne State University
Press, 1973.

699 *Life of the cheerful schoolmaster Maria Wutz*
(Leben des vergnügten Schulmeisterleins Maria Wuz).
Trans. John D. Grayson. In Flores, *Nineteenth
century German tales.*

700 See also: Francke, *The German classics*, IV.

701 KELLER, Gottfried.

The banner of the upright seven. Ursula (Das
Fähnlein der sieben Aufrechten. Ursula). Trans.
B.Q. Morgan. Introd. Gerda Breit. New York:
Ungar, 1974, pb. Cf. 703-04.

702 *Clothes make the man* (Kleider machen Leute). In
Steinhauer, *Twelve German novellas.*

703 *The company of the upright seven* (Das Fähnlein
der sieben Aufrechten). Trans. B.Q. Morgan. In
Francke, *The German classics*, XIV

704 *The flag of the company of seven* (Das Fähnlein
der sieben Aufrechten). Trans. J.R. Davies. In
Engel, *German narrative prose*, I.

705 *The governor of Greifensee* (Der Landvogt von
Greifensee). Trans. P.B. Thomas. In Francke,
The German classics, XIV.

KELLER (cont'd).

706   *Green Henry* (Der grüne Heinrich). Trans. A.M.
Holt. London: Calder; New York: Grove Press,
1960. Cf. 712.

707   *Legends and people.* Comps. J.I. Rodale and D.M.
Gilixon. Emmaus, Pa.: Rodale Books, 1953.

708   *Legends of long ago* (Sieben Legenden). Trans.
Charles Hart Handschin. Freeport, N.Y.: Books
for Libraries Press, 1970.

709   *A little legend of the dance* (Das Tanzlegendchen).
Trans. M.D. Hottinger. In Pick, *German stories
and tales.*

710   *A little legend of the dance.* Trans. M.D.
Hottinger. In Spender, *Great German short stories.*

711   *Martin Salander* (Martin Salander). Trans. Kenneth
Halwas. London: Calder, 1964.

712   *Meret* (excerpt from Der grüne Heinrich). Trans.
Mary Hottinger. In Flores, *Nineteenth century
German tales.*

713   *The misused love letters. Regula Amrain and her
youngest son* (Die missbrauchten Liebesbriefe.
Frau Regel Amrain). Trans. Michael Bullock and
Anne Fremantle. Introd. Michael Bullock. New
York: Ungar, 1974, pb.

714   *The naughty saint Vitalis.* In Lange, *Great German
short novels.*

715   *The naughty saint Vitalis.* Trans. Martin Wyness.
In Cerf, *Great German short novels and stories.*

KELLER (cont'd).

716   *Tne people of Seldwyla, and Seven legends* (Die Leute
      von Seldwyla. Sieben Legenden). Trans. M.D. Hottinger.
      Freeport, N.Y.: Books for Libraries Press, 1970 (1931).

717   *Seldwyla folks: Three singular tales* (Die Leute von
      Seldwyla). Trans. Wolf von Schierbrand. Free-
      port, N.Y.: Books for Libraries Press, 1971.

718   *Spiegel, the kitten* (Spiegel, das Kätzchen). In
      Kesten, *The blue flower*.

719   *Ursula* (Ursula). Trans. B.Q. Morgan. In Francke,
      The German classics, XIV.

720   *A village Romeo and Juliet* (Romeo und Julia auf
      dem Dorfe). Trans. Ronald Taylor. In Taylor,
      Three German classics.

721   *A village Romeo and Juliet*. Trans. Peter Tegel.
      London: Blackie, 1967.

722   *A village Romeo and Juliet*. Trans. Paul Bernard
      Thomas. Introd. Bayard Q. Morgan. London: Calder;
      New York: Ungar, 1955, 1960, pb.

723   *A village Romeo and Juliet*. Trans. P.B. Thomas.
      In Francke, *The German classics*, XIV.

724   See also: Thomas, *German verse*; Lamport, *German
      short stories*.

725   KLEIST, Heinrich von.
      Amphitryon: A comedy (Amphitryon). Trans. Marion
      Sonnenfeld. New York: Ungar, 1962, pb.

726   *The beggar-woman of Locarno* (Das Bettelweib von
      Locarno). Trans. E.N. Bennett. In Bennett,
      German short stories.

KLEIST (cont'd).

727   *The broken jug* (Der zerbrochene Krug). Trans.
Roger Jones. Manchester: Manchester University
Press, 1977, pb.

728   *The broken jug.* Trans. John T. Krumpelmann. New
York: Ungar, 1962, pb.

729   *The broken jug.* Trans. Lawrence P.R. Wilson. In
John Allan, ed., *Four continental plays* (London:
Heinemann, 1964).

730   *The broken pitcher* (Der zerbrochene Krug). Trans.
Bayard Q. Morgan. Chapel Hill, N.C.: University
of North Carolina Press, 1961; New York: AMS
Press, 1966.

731   *The earthquake in Chile* (Das Erdbeben in Chile).
In Kesten, *The blue flower.*

732   *The earthquake in Chile.* In Lange, *Great German
short novels.*

733   *The earthquake in Chile.* Trans. Michael Hamburger.
In Spender, *Great German short stories.*

734   *Kaethchen of Heilbronn* (Käthchen von Heilbronn).
Trans. F.E. Pierce. In Pierce/Schreiber, *Fiction
and fantasy.*

735   *Katie of Heilbronn.* Trans. Arthur H. Hughes.
Hartford: Trinity College, 1960.

736   *The marionette theatre* (Das Marionettentheater).
Trans. D. Gifford. In: M. Armitage, *Five essays
on Klee* (New York: Duell Sloan and Pearce, 1950).

KLEIST (cont'd).

737   *The marquise of O, and other stories.* Trans.
       Martin Greenberg. Pref. Thomas Mann. New York:
       Criterion Books, 1960; New American Library, 1962,
       pb; London: Faber and Faber, 1963; New York:
       Ungar, 1973, pb.

738   *The marquise of O, and other stories.* Trans.
       David Luke and Nigel Reeves. Harmondsworth,
       Baltimore: Penguin Books, 1978, pb.

739   *Michael Kohlhaas, and The marquise of O* (Michael
       Kohlhaas. Die Marquise von O,). Trans. Martin
       Greenberg. London: Sphere, 1969 (1963).

740   *Michael Kohlhaas.* Trans. F.H. King. In Kuno
       Francke, *The German classics,* IV.

741   *Michael Kohlhaas.* Trans. Janes Kirkup. London,
       Glasgow: Blackie, 1967.

742   *Michael Kohlhaas.* Trans. Charles E. Passage. In
       Flores, *Nineteenth century German tales.*

743   *Michael Kohlhaas.* Trans. Charles E. Passage. In
       Winner, *Great European short novels,* I.

744   *Michael Kohlhaas.* In Steinhauer, *Twelve German
       novellas.*

745   *Penthesilea* (Penthesilea). Trans. F.J. Lamport.
       In Lamport, *Five German tragedies.*

746   *Penthesilea.* Trans. Humphry Trevelyan. In
       Bentley, *The classic theatre.*

747   *Prince Frederick of Homburg* (Prinz Friedrich von
       Homburg). Trans. Martin Esslin. In Esslin,
       The genius of the German theater.

KLEIST (cont'd).

748   *Prince Frederick of Homburg.*   Trans. L. Robert
       Scheuer.   Great Neck, N.Y.: Barron, 1963, pb.

749   *Prince Frederick of Homburg.*   Trans. L. Robert
       Scheuer.   In Bentley, *The great playwrights*, I.

750   *Prince Friedrich of Homburg.*   Trans. James Kirkup.
       In Caputi, *Masterworks of world drama*, VI.

751   *The prince of Homburg.*   Trans. Hermann Hagedorn.
       In Kuno Francke, *The German classics*, IV.

752   *The prince of Homburg.*   Trans. James Kirkup.   In
       Bentley, *The classic theatre.*

753   *The prince of Homburg.*   Trans. Theodore H. Lustig.
       In Lustig, *Classical German drama.*

754   *The prince of Homburg.*   Trans. Charles E. Passage.
       New York: Liberal Arts, 1956.

755   *Saint Cecilia* (Die heilige Cäcilie).   Trans. J.F.
       Hargreaves and J.G. Cumming.   In Engel, *German
       narrative prose*, I.

756   See also: Lamport, *German short stories.*

757 KÖRNER, Theodor.
       Selections in: Francke, *The German classics*, V.

758 LASSALLE, Ferdinand.
       Selections in: Francke, *The German classics*, X.

759 LENAU, Nikolaus.
       Poems and letters.   Bilingual.   Trans. Winthrop
       H. Root.   New York: Ungar, 1964.

760   Selections in: Flores, *Anthology of German poetry*;
       Francke, *The German classics*, VII; Gode, *Anthology*

LENAU (cont'd).

of German poetry; MacInnes, *A collection of German verse*; Thomas, *German verse*; Broicher, *German lyrics and ballads*.

761 LILIENCRON, Detlev von.
Selections in: Francke, *The German classics*, XVIII: Deutsch, *Contemporary German poetry*; Bithell, *Contemporary German poetry*.

762 LUDWIG, Otto.
Between heaven and earth (Zwischen Himmel und Erde). Trans. Muriel Almon. In Kuno Francke, *The German classics*, IX.

763 *Between heaven and earth*. Trans. (abridged) Muriel Almon. Introd. Paul Weigand. New York: Ungar, 1965, pb.

764 *The hereditary forester* (Der Erbförster). Trans. Alfred Remy. In Kuno Francke, *The German classics*, IX.

765 MACKAY, John Henry.
The anarchists (Die Anarchisten). Trans. George Schumm. Boston: Tucker, 1891; New York: Revisionist Press, 1976.

766 MEYER, Conrad Ferdinand.
The complete narrative prose. Trans. George F. Folkers, David B. Dickens, and Marion W. Sonnenfeld. Introd. George F. Folkers. 2 vols. Lewisburg, Pa.: Bucknell University Press, 1977.

767 *The monk's marriage* (Die Hochzeit des Mönchs). Trans. W.G. Howard. In Francke, *The German classics*, XIV. Cf. 770.

MEYER (cont'd).

768 *Plautus in the convent* (Plautus im Nonnenkloster).
Trans. W.G. Howard. In Francke, *The German classics*, XIV.

769 *Plautus in the convent.* In Lange, *Great German
short novels.*

770 *Plautus in the convent. The monk's marriage.*
Trans. William Guild Howard. Introd. Konrad
Schaum. New York: Ungar, 1965, pb.

771 *The saint* (Der Heilige). Trans. Edward Franklin
Hauch. New York: Simon and Schuster, 1930.

772 *The saint.* Trans. W.F. Twaddell. Providence, R.I.:
Brown University Press, 1977.

773 *The sufferings of a boy* (Die Leiden eines Knaben).
In Steinhauer, *Twelve German novellas.*

774 *The tempting of Pescara* (Die Versuchung des
Pescara). Trans. Clara Bell. New York: Gotts-
berger, 1890; New York: Fertig, 1975.

775 Selections in: Francke, *The German classics*, XIV;
Broicher, *German lyrics and ballads*; Gode, *Antho-
logy of German poetry*; MacInnes, *A collection of
German verse*; Thomas, *German verse*; Kaufmann,
Twenty-five German poets.

776 MÖRIKE, Eduard.
Poems. Bilingual. Trans. Norah K. Cruickshank
and Gilbert F. Cunningham. London: Methuen, 1959.

777 *Mozart on his way to Prague* (Mozart auf der Reise
nach Prag). Trans. Mary Hottinger. In Flores,
Nineteenth century German tales.

MORIKE (cont'd).

778   *Mozart on the way to Prague.* Trans. Walter and
       Catherine Alison Phillips. New York: Pantheon,
       1947.

779   *Mozart's journey from Vienna to Prague.* Trans.
       Florence Leonard. In Kuno Francke, *The German
       classics*, VII.

780   *Mozart's journey to Prague.* Trans. Leopold von
       Loewenstein-Wertheim. London: Calder, 1957, 1976,
       pb; New York: British Book Centre, 1958.

781   Selections in: Flores, *Anthology of German poetry*;
       Francke, *The German classics*, VII; Broicher,
       German lyrics and ballads; Forster, *Penguin German
       verse*; Gode, *Anthology of German poetry*; MacInnes,
       A collection of German verse; Thomas, *German verse*.

782   See also: *Friedrich Hölderlin and Eduard Mörike:
       Selected poems*, trans. Christopher Middleton
       (Chicago, London: University of Chicago Press,
       1972). Bilingual.

783 MOLTKE, Helmuth von.
       Selections in: Francke, *The German classics*, X.

784 NESTROY, Johann.
       *Three comedies: A man full of nothing. The talis-
       man. Love affairs and wedding bells.* Trans. Max
       Knight and Joseph Fabry. Foreword Thornton Wilder.
       New York: Ungar, 1967, pb.

785   *The matchmaker* (Einen Jux will er sich machen).
       New York: French, 1957.

786 NIETZSCHE, Friedrich.
     Complete works. Ed. Oscar Levy. New York:
     Russell and Russell, 1964 (1909), 18 vols.

787 *A Nietzsche reader*. Trans. R.J. Hollingdale.
     New York: Penguin Books, 1978, pb.

788 *The portable Nietzsche*. Ed. Walter Kaufmann.
     New York: Viking Press, 1954, 1960, pb.

789 *Beyond good and evil* (Jenseits von Gut und Böse).
     Trans. Marianne Cowan. Chicago: Regnery, 1959, pb.

790 *Beyond good and evil*. Trans. R.J. Hollingdale.
     Harmondsworth: Penguin, 1973, pb.

791 *Beyond good and evil*. Trans. Walter Kaufmann.
     New York: Random, 1966, pb.

792 *The birth of tragedy*. *The genealogy of morals*
     (Die Geburt der Tragödie. Zur Genealogie der
     Moral). Trans. Francis Golffing. New York:
     Doubleday, 1956, pb.

793 *The birth of tragedy*. *The case of Wagner* (Die
     Geburt der Tragödie. Der Fall Wagner). Trans.
     Walter Kaufmann. New York: Random, 1967, pb.

794 *Ecce homo* (Ecce homo). Trans. R.J. Hollingdale.
     Harmondsworth: Penguin, 1979, pb.

795 *The genealogy of morals*. *Ecce homo* (Zur Genea-
     logie der Moral. Ecce homo). Trans. Walter
     Kaufmann. New York: Random, 1967, pb.

796 *Joyful wisdom* (Die fröhliche Wissenschaft). Trans.
     Thomas Common (1909). New York: Ungar, 1960.

NIETZSCHE (cont'd).

797 *Philosophy in the tragic age of the Greeks* (Die
Philosophie im tragischen Zeitalter der Griechen).
Trans. Marianne Cowan. Chicago: Regnery, 1962, pb.

798 *Schopenhauer as educator* (Schopenhauer als Erzieher). Trans. James W. Hillesheim. Chicago:
Regnery, 1965, pb.

799 *Thus spake Zarathustra* (Also sprach Zarathustra).
Trans. Marianne Cowan. Chicago: Regnery, 1956.

800 *Thus spoke Zarathustra*. Trans. R.J. Hollingdale.
Harmondsworth, Baltimore: Penguin, 1961, 1976, pb.

801 *Thus spoke Zarathustra*. Trans. Walter Kaufmann.
New York: Viking Press, 1966, pb.

802 *Thus spake Zarathustra*. Trans. A. Kille and M.M.
Bozman. Introd. Roy Pascal. London: Dent; New
York: Dutton, 1958, 1972, pb.

803 *Twilight of the idols. The anti-Christ* (Götzen-
Dämmerung. Der Antichrist). Trans. R.J. Hollingdale. Harmondsworth: Penguin, 1968, 1978, pb.

804 *The use and abuse of history* (Unzeitgemässe
Betrachtungen). Trans. Adrian Collins. Introd.
Julius Kraft. New York: Liberal Arts, 1957.

805 *The will to power* (Der Wille zur Macht). Trans.
Walter Kaufmann. New York: Random, 1968, pb.

806 *Unpublished letters*. Ed. and trans. Kurt F.
Leidecker. New York: Philosophical Library,
1959; London: Owen, 1960.

807 Selections in: Francke, *The German classics*, XV;
Thomas, *German verse*; Kaufmann, *Twenty-five German
poets*.

808 NOVALIS.

Henry von Ofterdingen (Heinrich von Ofterdingen).
Trans. Palmer Hilty. New York: Ungar, 1964, pb.

809 Hyacinth and Rosebud. Eros and Fabel (Hyazinth
und Rosenblüte). Trans. Florence Bryan and Kathe
Roth. Aberdeen: Selma Publ., 1955.

810 Hymns to the night (Hymnen an die Nacht). Bilingual.
Trans. M. Cotterell. Introd. August Closs.
London: Phoenix House, 1948; Hollywood-by-the-sea,
Fla.: Transatlantic Arts, 1949.

811 Hymns to the night, and other selected writings.
Trans. Charles E. Passage. New York: Bobbs-
Merrill, 1960, pb.

812 The novices of Sais (Die Lehrlinge von Saïs).
Trans. Ralph Manheim. Introd. Stephen Spender.
New York: Valentin, 1949.

813 Sacred songs. Trans. Eileen Hutchins. Aberdeen:
Selma Publ., 1956.

814 Selections in: Flores, Anthology of German poetry;
Francke, The German classics, IV; Thomas, German
verse; Kaufmann, Twenty-five German poets.

815 PLATEN, August Graf von.
Selections in: Flores, Anthology of German poetry;
Francke, The German classics, V; Broicher, German
lyrics and ballads; Thomas, German verse.

816 POLENZ, Wilhelm von.
Selections in: Francke, The German classics,
XVII.

817 RAABE, Wilhelm.

Else von der Tanne. Bilingual. Trans. and ed.
J.C. O'Flaherty and Janet K. King. University,
Ala.: University of Alabama Press, 1972.

818 *The hunger pastor* (Der Hungerpastor). Trans.
Muriel Almon. In Kuno Francke, *The German
classics*, XI.

819 RAIMUND, Ferdinand.

Spendthrift: A musical fairy tale in three acts
(Der Verschwender). Trans. Erwin Tramer. New
York: Ungar, 1949.

820 REUTER, Fritz.

The Bräsig episodes from 'Ut mine Stromtid.'
Trans. M.W. Macdowall. Rev. E. von Mach. In
Kuno Francke, *The German classics*, VIII.

821 RICHTER, Johann Paul Friedrich.
See: JEAN PAUL.

822 RIEHL, W.H.
Selections in: Francke, *The German classics*, VIII.

823 ROSEGGER, Peter.
Selections in: Francke, *The German classics*, XVI.

824 RÜCKERT, Friedrich.
Selections in: Francke, *The German classics*, V;
Thomas, *German verse*.

825 SACHER-MASOCH, Leopold von.
Venus in furs (Venus im Pelz). Trans. J. Brownell.
New York: Faro, 1931.

826 *Venus in furs*. Trans. Jean McNeil. In Gilles
Deleuze, *Sacher-Masoch: An interpretation,* trans.
Jean McNeil (London: Faber, 1971).

SACHER-MASOCH (cont'd).

827   *Venus in furs.* New York: Privately printed for
the Sylvan Press, 1947.

828   *Venus in furs.* London: Sphere Books, 1969, pb.

829   *Venus in furs.* Trans. John Glassco. Burnaby,
B.C.: Blackfish Press, 1977.

830 SCHEFFEL, Joseph Victor von.
Ekkehard (Ekkehard). Trans. Sophie Delffs (1872).
In Francke, *The German classics*, XIII.

831   *Ekkehard: A novel.* Trans. (abridged) Sofie Delffs
(1872). Introd. Gerard F. Schmidt. New York:
Ungar, 1965, pb.

832   Further selections in: Francke, *The German classics*, XIII.

833 SCHENKENDORF, Maximilian Gottfried von.
Selections in: Francke, *The German classics*, V.

834 SCHLAF, Johannes, and Arno Holz.
A death. Trans. J.R. Davies. In Engel, *German
narrative prose*, I.

835 SCHLEGEL, August Wilhelm.
Lectures on dramatic art (Über dramatische Kunst
und Literatur). Trans. John Black. In Kuno
Francke, *The German classics*, IV.

836 SCHLEGEL, Friedrich.
Aphorisms. Trans. L.H. Gray. In Kuno Francke,
The German classics, IV.

837   *Dialogue on poetry, and Literary aphorisms.* Trans.
Ernst Behler and Roman Struc. University Park:
Pennsylvania State University Press, 1968.

SCHLEGEL, F. (cont'd).

838   *Literary Notebooks 1797-1801.* London: Athlone, 1957.

839   *Lucinde, and The fragments* (Lucinde). Trans. Peter Firchow. Minneapolis: University of Minnesota Press; London: Oxford University Press, 1971.

840   *Lucinda.* Trans. P.B. Thomas. In Kuno Francke, *The German classics,* IV.

841 SCHLEIERMACHER, Friedrich.
       The Christian faith. Trans. H.R. Mackintosh and J.S. Stewart. New York: Scribner, 1928.

842   *On religion* (Über die Religion). Trans. T.N. Tice. Richmond: John Knox Press, 1969.

843   *On religion: Speeches to its cultured despisers.* Introd. and abridged E.G. Waring. Trans. John Oman. New York: Ungar, 1955, pb; New York: Harper, 1958.

844   Selections in: Francke, *The German classics,* V.

845 SCHÖNHERR, Karl.
       Faith and fireside (Glaube und Heimat). Trans. E. von Mach. New York, 1913-15.

846   Selections in: Francke, *The German classics,* XVI.

847 SCHOPENHAUER, Arthur.
       The works of Schopenhauer. Sel. and ed. Will Durant. Trans. T.B. Saunders, R.B. Haldane, John Kemp. New York: Simon and Schuster, 1928.

848   *Essays and aphorisms.* Trans. R.J. Hollingdale. Baltimore: Penguin, 1970.

SCHOPENHAUER (cont'd).

849 *The world as will and representation* (Die Welt
als Wille und Vorstellung). Trans. E.F.J. Payne.
Indian Hills, Colo.: Falcon's Wing Press, 1958, pb.

850 Selections in: Francke, *The German classics*, XV.

851 SCHUMANN, Robert.
*The musical world of Robert Schumann: A selection
from his own writings* (Letters). Trans. Henry
Pleasants. London: Gollancz, 1965.

852 SEIDEL, Heinrich.
Selections in: Francke, *The German classics*, XIII.

853 SPIELHAGEN, Friedrich.
Storm flood (Sturmflut). Trans. M.D. Learned.
In Kuno Francke, *The German classics*, XI.

854 STIFTER, Adalbert.
Selections. Ed. K. Spalding. London: Macmillan,
1952.

855 *Abdias* (Abdias). Trans. N.C. Wormleighton and
H. Mayer. In Engel, *German narrative prose*, I.

856 *Brigitta* (Brigitta). Trans. Ilsa Barea. In
Spender, *Great German short stories.*

857 *Brigitta.* Trans. Edward Fitzgerald. London,
Emmaus, Pa.: Rodale Press, 1957.

858 *Brigitta.* Trans. Herman Salinger. In Flores,
Nineteenth century German tales.

859 *Limestone, and other stories.* Trans. David Luke.
New York: Harcourt, Brace and World, 1968. (Limestone; Tourmaline; The doorkeeper; The recluse).

STIFTER (cont'd).

860 *The recluse* (Der Hagestolz). Trans. David Luke.
London: Jonathan Cape, 1968.

861 *Rock-crystal* (Bergkristall). Bilingual. Trans.
J.R. Forster. London: Harrap, 1950.

862 *Rock crystal.* Trans. Lee M. Hollander. In Kuno
Francke, *The German classics* , VIII.

863 *Rock crystal.* Trans. Elizabeth Mayer and Marianne
Moore. In Pick, *German stories and tales.*

864 *Rock crystal, A Christmas tale.* Trans. Elizabeth
Mayer and Marianne Moore. New York: Pantheon,
1945, 1965.

865 STORM, Theodor.
The rider on the white horse, and selected stories.
Trans. James Wright. New York: New American
Library, 1964, pb. Cf. 871-72, 875-76.

866 *Aquis submersus* (Aquis submersus). Trans. J.
Millar. Glasgow, 1910. Cf. 876.

867 *Immensee* (Immensee). Trans. C.W. Bell. In Cerf,
Great German short novels and stories.

868 *Immensee.* Trans. G. Reinhardt. Great Neck, N.Y.:
Barron, 1950, pb.

869 *Immensee.* Trans. Ronald Taylor. In Taylor, *Three
German classics.*

870 *Immensee.* In Lange, *Great German short novels.*

871 *The rider of the white horse* (Der Schimmelreiter).
Trans. Muriel Almon. In Kuno Francke, *The German
classics*, XI.

STORM (cont'd).

872 *The rider on the white horse.* Trans. Muriel Almon.
In Mornin, *Three eerie tales.* Cf. 865, 875-76.

873 *The senator's sons* (Die Söhne des Senators).
Trans. J.M. South. In Engel, *German narrative
prose*, I.

874 *Viola tricolor. Curator Carsten* (Viola Tricolor.
Carsten Curator). Trans. B.Q. Morgan and F.M.
Voigt. New York: Ungar, 1956, pb; London:
Calder, 1956, 1963.

875 *The white horse rider* (Der Schimmelreiter). Trans.
Stella Humphries. London, Glasgow: Blackie, 1966.

876 *The white horseman. Beneath the flood* (Der Schimmelreiter. Aquis submersus). Trans. Geoffrey
Skelton. London: New English Library, 1962, pb.

877 Selections in: Francke, *The German classics*, XI;
Broicher, *German lyrics and ballads*; Forster,
Penguin German verse; Gode, *Anthology of German
poetry*; Thomas, *German verse.*

878 See also: Lamport, *German short stories.*

879 STRACHWITZ, Moritz Graf von.
Selections in: Francke, *The German classics*, VII.

880 SUDERMANN, Hermann.
Honor (Die Ehre). Trans. H.R. Bankhage. New
York, 1915.

881 *The Indian lily, and other stories* (Die indische
Lilie). Trans. Ludwig Lewisohn (1911). Freeport,
N.Y.: Books for Libraries Press, 1970.

SUDERMANN (cont'd).

882   *Iolanthe's wedding* (Jolanthes Hochzeit). Trans.
Adele Seltzer (1918). Freeport, N.Y.: Books for
Libraries Press, 1970.

883   *John the Baptist* (Johannes). Trans. B. Marshall
(1909). In Francke, *The German classics*, XVII.

884   *John the Baptist*. Trans. B. Marshall. London,
New York: 1909.

885   *The joy of living* (Es lebe das Leben). Trans.
E. Wharton. London, New York, 1902.

886   *A man and his picture* (Sodoms Ende). Trans.
anon. London, 1903.

887   *Morituri* (Morituri). Trans. A. Alexander. New
York, 1910; London, 1912.

888   *St. John's fire* (Johannisfeuer). Trans. C. and
H.T. Porter. Boston, 1904.

889   See also: Cerf, *Great German short novels and
stories*.

890   TIECK, Ludwig.
Auburn Egbert (Der blonde Eckbert). In Kesten,
The blue flower.

891   *Blond Eckbert* (Der blonde Eckbert). Trans. Helene
Scher. In Scher, *Four romantic tales*. Cf. 893.

892   *The elves* (Die Elfen). Trans. F.H. Hedge. In
Kuno Francke, *The German classics*, IV.

893   *Fair Eckbert* (Der blonde Eckbert). Trans. P.B.
Thomas. In Kuno Francke, *The German classics*,
IV.

TIECK (cont'd).

894   *Der gestiefelte Kater/Puss-in-Boots.* Bilingual.
Trans. and ed. Gerald Gillespie. Edinburgh:
Edinburgh University Press, 1974, pb.

895   *Life's luxuries* (Des Lebens Überfluss). Trans.
E.N. Bennett. In Bennett, *German short stories.*

896   *Life's superfluence* (Des Lebens Überfluss). Trans.
Ian Hilton. In Engel, *German narrative prose*, I.

897   *Puss in boots* (Der gestiefelte Kater). Trans.
Lillie Winter. In Kuno Francke, *The German
classics*, IV.

898   *The runenberg* (Der Runenberg). Trans. Thomas
Carlyle. In Pierce/Schreiber, *Fiction and fantasy.*

899   and W.H. Wackenroder. *Outpourings of an art-loving
friar* (Herzensergiessungen eines kunstliebenden
Klosterbruders). Trans. Edward Mornin. New York:
Ungar, 1975, pb.

900 UHLAND, Johann Ludwig.
Selections in: Francke, *The German classics*, V;
Roberts, *Treasury of German ballads*; Thomas,
German verse; Kaufmann, *Twenty-five German poets.*

901 WACKENRODER, Wilhelm Heinrich.
Confessions and fantasies. Ed. and trans. Mary
Hurst Schubert. University Park and London:
Pennsylvania State University Press, 1971.

902   Selections in: Pierce/Schreiber, *Fiction and fantasy.*

903   and Ludwig Tieck. *Outpourings of an art-loving
friar.* Trans. Edward Mornin. New York: Ungar,
1975, pb.

904 WAGNER, Richard.

Complete operas. Trans. E. Newman and others. Leipzig, 1914.

905 *My life* (Mein Leben). London: Constable, 1911, 2 vols.

906 *Prose works.* Trans. W.A. Ellis. Saint Clair Shores, Mi.: Scholarly Press, 1972 (1893-99), 8 vols.

907 *The ring of the Nibelung* (Der Ring des Nibelungen). Bilingual. Trans. Andrew Porter. London: Faber, 1977, pb.

908 *The ring of the Nibelung.* Bilingual. Trans. Stewart Robb. Introd. Edward Downes. New York: Dutton, 1960, pb.

909 *Tristan and Isolde* (Tristan and Isolde). Bilingual. Ed. and trans. Stewart Robb. New York: Dutton, 1965, pb.

910 Selections in: Francke, *The German classics*, XV.

911 WERNER, Zacharias.

Sons of the valley. (Die Söhne des Tals). Selections. Trans. E. Lewis. In Bates, *German drama*, III.

912 *The twenty-fourth of February* (Der vierundzwanzigste Februar). Trans. W.H.H. Chambers. In Bates, *German drama*, I.

913 WIDMANN, Joseph Victor.

Selections in: Francke, *The German classics*, XIV.

914 WILBRANDT, Adolf.

Selections in: Francke, *The German classics*, XVI.

915 WILDENBRUCH, Ernst von.

Selections in: Francke, *The German classics*, XVII.

916 WILHELM II, Emperor.

Selections in: Francke, *The German classics*, XV.

917 ZSCHOKKE, Heinrich.

The bravo of Venice: A romance (Aballino, der grosse Bandit). Trans. M.G. Lewis (1805). Ed. Devendra P. Varma. New York: Arno Press, 1972.

V Twentieth century

918 AICHINGER, Ilse.
The bound man (Der Gefesselte). Trans. Eric
Mosbacher. In Spender, *Great German short stories.*

919 *The bound man, and other stories* (Der Gefesselte:
Erzählungen). Trans. Eric Mosbacher. London:
Secker and Warburg, 1955; New York: Noonday Press,
1956; Freeport, N.Y.: Books for Libraries Press,
1971.

920 *Herod's children.* Trans. Cornelia Schaeffer.
New York: Athenaum Publ., 1963.

921 *Selected short stories and dialogs.* Ed. James
C. Alldridge. Oxford, New York: Pergamon Press,
1966.

922 See also: Newnham, *German short stories.*

923 ANDERSCH, Alfred.
Ephraim's book (Efraim). Trans. Ralph Manheim.
Garden City, N.Y.: Doubleday, 1970; London: Cape,
1972.

924 *Flight to afar* (Sansibar, oder der letzte Grund).
Trans. Michael Bullock. London: Gollancz; New
York: Coward-McCann, 1958; Bath: Cedric Chivers
Ltd., 1971.

ANDERSCH (cont'd).

925   *My disappearance in Providence, and other stories*
(Mein Verschwinden in Providence). Trans. Ralph
Manheim. New York: Doubleday, 1978.

926   *The night of the giraffe, and other stories* (In
der Nacht der Giraffe). Trans. Christa Armstrong.
New York: Pantheon Books, 1964; London: Murray,
1965.

927   *The redhead* (Die Rote). Trans. Michael Bullock.
London: Heinemann; New York: Pantheon Books, 1961;
Popular Library, 1962, pb.

928   *Winterspelt.* Trans. Richard and Clara Winston.
New York: Doubleday, 1978.

929 ANDRES, Stefan.
We are God's Utopia (Wir sind Utopia). Trans.
Elita Walker Caspari. Chicago: Regnery, 1957, pb.

930   *We are Utopia* (Wir sind Utopia). Trans. Cyrus
Brooks. London: Gollancz, 1955.

931 APITZ, Bruno.
Naked among wolves (Nackt unter Wölfen). Trans.
Edith Anderson. Berlin: Seven Seas Publ.; London:
Collets, 1960, 1967.

932 ARP, Hans.
Dreams and projects. Bilingual. Trans. Ralph
Manheim. New York: Valentin, 1952.

933   Selections in: Watts, *Three painter-poets*; Hamburger, *Modern German poetry*; Hamburger, *German
poetry 1910-1975.*

934   BACHMANN, Ingeborg.

The thirtieth year (Das dreissigste Jahr). Trans.
Michael Bullock. London: Deutsch; New York:
Knopf, 1964.

935   Selections in: Rothenberg, *New young German poets*;
Bridgwater, *Twentieth-century German verse*;
Hamburger, *German poetry 1910-1975*.

936   BAHR, Hermann.

The master (Der Meister). Trans. B.F. Glazer.
New York, 1918.

937   BARLACH, Ernst.

Squire Blue Boll (Der blaue Boll). Trans. J.M.
Ritchie. In Ritchie/Garten, *Seven expressionist
plays*.

938   *Three plays*. Trans. Alex Page. Minneapolis:
University of Minnesota Press; London: Oxford
University Press, 1964. (The flood; The genuine
Sedemunds; The blue Boll).

939   BARTSCH, Kurt.

Selections in Hamburger, *East German poetry*.

940   BARTSCH, Rudolf Hans.

The Styrian wine-carter (Der steirische Wein-
fuhrmann). Trans. B.Q. Morgan. In Francke, *The
German classics*, XIX.

941   BAUER, Walter.

The price of morning: Selected poems. Bilingual.
Trans., introd. and ed. Henry Beissel. Vancouver:
Prism International Press, 1968.

BAUER, Walter (cont'd).

942   *A different sun.* Trans. Henry Beissel. Ottawa:
       Oberon Books, 1976.

943   *A slight trace of ash: Poems of recollection.*
       Trans. Humphrey Milnes. Toronto: R. Ascham
       Press, 1976.

944   BAUER, Wolfgang.
       Change, and other plays. Trans. Martin and Renata
       Esslin, Herb Greer. New York: Hill and Wang;
       London: Calder and Boyars, 1973 (British edn.: *All
       change*).

945   *Shakespeare the sadist* (Shakespeare der Sadist).
       Trans. Renata and Martin Esslin. London: Eyre
       Methuen, 1977, pb. (Also contains: Fassbinder,
       Bremen coffee; Handke, My foot my tutor; Kroetz,
       Stallerhof).

946   BECHER, Johannes R.
       Farewell (Abschied). Trans. Joan Becker. Berlin:
       Seven Seas Publ., 1970.

947   BECKER, Jurek.
       Jacob the liar (Jakob der Lügner). Trans. Melvin
       Kornfeld. New York: Harcourt Brace Jovanovich,
       1975; London: Harcourt Brace Jovanovich, 1976.

948   BEER-HOFMANN, Richard.
       Jacob's dream (Jaakobs Traum). Trans. I.B. Wynn.
       New York, 1946.

949   BENDER, Hans.
       See: Newnham, *German short stories.*

950 BENN, Gottfried.

The conquest. Trans. Christopher Middleton. In Spender, *Great German short stories.*

951 *Primal vision: Selected writings* (Primäre Tage). Trans. W. Hasenclever. Ed. E.B. Ashton. New York: New Directions, 1960, pb; London: Bodley Head, 1961; London: Marion Boyars, 1976.

952 Selections in: Bridgwater, *Twentieth-century German verse*; Hamburger, *Modern German poetry*; Hamburger, *German poetry 1910-1975*; Schwebell, *Contemporary German poetry*; Kaufmann, *Twenty-five German poets.*

953 BERGENGRUEN, Werner.

Experience on an island (Erlebnis auf einer Insel). Trans. Lawrence Wilson. In Yuill, *German narrative prose*, II.

954 *The last captain of horse: A portrait of chivalry* (Der letzte Rittmeister). Trans. Eric Peters. London, New York: Thames and Hudson, 1953; New York: Vanguard, 1954.

955 *A matter of conscience* (Der Grosstyrann und das Gericht). Trans. Norman Cameron. London, New York: Thames and Hudson, 1952.

956 *Ordeal by fire* (Die Feuerprobe). In Steinhauer, *Twelve German novellas.*

957 BERGER, Uwe.

Selections in: Deicke, *Time for dreams.*

958 BERNHARD, Thomas.

The force of habit: A comedy (Die Macht der Gewohnheit). Trans. Neville and Stephen Plaice. London: Heinemann Educational, 1976, pb.

BERNHARD (cont'd),

959   *Gargoyles* (Verstörung). Trans. Richard and Clara
Winston. New York: Knopf, 1970.

960   *The lime works* (Das Kalkwerk). Trans. Sophie
Wilkins. New York: Knopf, 1973.

961   Selections in: Schwebell, *Contemporary German
poetry.*

962 BICHSEL, Peter.
*And really Frau Blum would very much like to meet
the milkman: Twenty-one short stories* (Eigentlich
möchte Frau Blum den Milchmann kennenlernen).
Trans. Michael Hamburger. London: Calder and
Boyars, 1968; New York: Delacorte Press, 1969.

963   *There's no such place as America* (Kindergeschichten).
Trans. Michael Hamburger. New York: Delacorte
Press, 1970.

964 BIENEK, Horst.
Bakunin, an invention (Bakunin, eine Invention).
Trans. Ralph R. Read. London: Gollancz, 1977.

965   *The cell* (Die Zelle). Trans. Ursula Mahlendorf.
Santa Barbara: Unicorn, 1972; Toronto: McClelland
and Stewart, 1973; London: Gollancz, 1974.

966   and Johannes Bobrowski. *Selected poems.* Trans.
Ruth E. and Matthew Mead. Harmondsworth: Penguin, 1971, pb.

967 BIERMANN, Wolf.
Poems and ballads. Trans. Steve Gooch. London:
Pluto, 1977.

BIERMANN (cont'd).

968 *The wire harp: Ballads, poems, songs* (Die Draht-
harfe). Trans. Eric Bentley. New York: Harcourt,
Brace and World, 1968, pb.

969 Selections in: Hamburger, *East German poetry.*

970 BIRKENFELD, Gunther.
A room in Berlin (Dritter Hof links). Trans.
Eric Sutton. New York: Avon, 1955.

971 BOBROWSKI, Johannes.
From the rivers. Trans. Ruth and Matthew Mead.
London: Anvil Press Poetry, 1975, pb.

972 *I taste bitterness.* Trans. Marc Linder. Berlin:
Seven Seas Publ., 1970.

973 *Levin's mill* (Levins Mühle). Trans. Janet Cropper.
London: Calder and Boyars, 1970.

974 and Horst Bienek. *Selected poems.* Trans. Ruth E.
and Matthew Mead. Harmondsworth: Penguin, 1971, pb.

975 *Shadow land: Selected poems* (Schattenland Ströme).
Trans. Ruth and Matthew Mead. Denver: Swallow,
1966; London: D. Carroll, 1967.

976 Selections in: Hamburger, *German poetry 1910-
1975*; Hamburger, *East German poetry*; Deicke, *Time
for dreams.*

977 BÖLL, Heinrich.
Eighteen stories. Trans. Leila Vennewitz. New
York: McGraw-Hill, 1966, 1971, pb.

978 *Absent without leave, and other stories* (Entfernung
von der Truppe; Als der Krieg ausbrach). Trans.

116

BÖLL (cont'd).

Leila Vennewitz. New York: McGraw-Hill, 1965,
1975; London: Weidenfeld and Nicolson, 1967;
London: Calder and Boyars, 1972, pb.

979   *Acquainted with the night* (Und sagte kein einziges
Wort). Trans. Richard Graves. New York: Holt,
Rinehart and Winston, 1954; London: Hutchinson,
1955.

980   *Adam, where art thou?* (Wo warst du, Adam?).
Trans. Mervyn Savill. New York: Criterion Books;
London: Arco Publ., 1955.

981   *Adam, and The train* (Wo warst du, Adam?; Der Zug
war pünktlich). Trans. Leila Vennewitz. New
York: McGraw, 1970, pb. Cf. 997-98.

982   *And where were you, Adam?* (Wo warst du, Adam?).
Trans. Leila Vennewitz. London: Secker and
Warburg, 1973, 1974; Harmondsworth: Penguin, 1978,
pb.

983   *Billiards at half past nine* (Billard um halbzehn).
Trans. Patrick Bowles. London: Weidenfeld and
Nicolson, 1961; New York: McGraw-Hill, 1962;
London: J. Calder, 1965.

984   *Billiards at half-past nine*. Trans. Leila
Vennewitz. New York: Avon Books, 1975, pb.

985   *Billiards at half-past nine*. Trans. Leila
Vennewitz. New York: New American Library, 1965.

986   *The bread of our early years* (Das Brot der frühen
Jahre). Trans. Mervyn Savill. London: Arco Publ.,
1957.

BÖLL (cont'd).

987   *The bread of those early years* (Das Brot der
       frühen Jahre). Trans. Leila Vennewitz. London:
       Secker and Warburg, 1976.

988   *Children are civilians too* (1947 bis 1951: Selec-
       tions). Trans. Leila Vennewitz. Toronto, New
       York: McGraw-Hill, 1970, pb; London: Secker and
       Warburg, 1973; Harmondsworth: Penguin, 1976, pb.

989   *The clown* (Ansichten eines Clowns). Trans. Leila
       Vennewitz. London: Weidenfeld and Nicolson: New
       York: McGraw-Hill, 1965, pb; Avon Books, n.d., pb;
       New York: New American Library, 1966; London:
       Calder and Boyars, 1972, pb.

990   *The end of a mission* (Ende einer Dienstfahrt).
       Trans. Leila Vennewitz. New York: McGraw-Hill,
       1967; London: Weidenfeld and Nicolson, 1968;
       Harmondsworth: Penguin, 1973, pb.

991   *Group portrait with lady* (Gruppenbild mit Dame).
       Trans. Leila Vennewitz. New York: McGraw-Hill;
       London: Secker and Warburg, 1973; New York: Avon,
       n.d., pb; Harmondsworth: Penguin, 1976, pb.

992   *Irish journal* (Irisches Tagebuch). Trans. Leila
       Vennewitz. New York: McGraw, 1967, pb.

993   *The lost honour of Katharina Blum* (Die verlorene
       Ehre der Katharina Blum). Trans. Leila Vennewitz.
       London: Secker and Warburg; New York: McGraw-Hill,
       1975.

994   *The man with the knives* (Der Mann mit den Messern).
       Trans. Richard Graves. In Spender, *Great German
       short stories*.

BÖLL (cont'd).

995   *Missing persons, and other essays* (Gesammelte
       Essays). Trans. Leila Vennewitz. New York:
       McGraw-Hill; London: Secker and Warburg, 1977.

996   *Tomorrow and yesterday* (Haus ohne Hüter). New
       York: Criterion Books, 1957. Cf. 1000.

997   *The train was on time* (Der Zug war pünktlich).
       Trans. Leila Vennewitz. London: Secker and
       Warburg, 1973; Harmondsworth: Penguin, 1979, pb.

998   *The train was on time* (Der Zug was pünktlich).
       Trans. Richard Graves. New York: Criterion
       Books; London: Arco Publ., 1956; London: Sphere
       Books, 1967.

999   *Traveller, if you come to Spa* (Wanderer kommst du
       nach Spa). Trans. Mervyn Savill. London: Arco
       Publ., 1956.

1000   *The unguarded house* (Haus ohne Hüter). Trans.
       Mervyn Savill. London: Arco Publ., 1957. Cf. 996.

1001   See also: Kaufmann, *Twenty-five German poets*;
       Lamport, *German short stories*; Newnham, *German
       short stories*.

1002   BONHOEFFER, Dietrich.
       Letters and papers from prison (Widerstand und
       Ergebung). Trans. Reginald H. Fuller. Ed.
       Eberhard Bethge. New York: Macmillan, 1953,
       1973, pb; London: Fontana Books, 1959, 1962, pb.

1003   BORCHERT, Wolfgang.
       The man outside: The prose works. Trans. David
       Porter. London: Hutchinson, 1952; Calder and Boy-
       ars, 1966; New York: New Directions, 1971.

BORCHERT (cont'd).

1004   *The dandelion* (Die Hundeblume). Trans. Richard
       Thonger. In Yuill, *German narrative prose*, II.

1005   *The outsider* (Draussen vor der Tür). Trans.
       Michael Benedikt. In Benedikt/Wellwarth, *Postwar
       German theatre*.

1006   *The sad geraniums and other stories* (Die traurigen
       Geranien). Trans. Keith Hamnett. New York: Ecco
       Press, 1973; London: Calder and Boyars, 1974.

1007   See also: Newnham, *German short stories*.

1008   BRAUN, Volker.
       Selections in: Hamburger, *East German poetry*;
       Deicke, *Time for dreams*.

1009   BRECHT, Bertolt.
       Collected plays: Volume 1. Ed. John Willett and
       Ralph Manheim. Various translators. London:
       Methuen, 1970; New York: Vintage Books; Pantheon,
       1971, pb. (Baal; Drums in the night; In the
       jungle of cities; Edward II; A respectable wed-
       ding; The beggar, or The dead dog; Driving out
       a devil; Lux in tenebris; The catch).

1010   *Collected plays: Volume 2, part 1.* Ed. John
       Willett and Ralph Manheim. London: Eyre Methuen,
       1979, pb. (Man equals man; The elephant calf).

1011   *Collected plays: Volume 2, part 2.* Ed. John
       Willett and Ralph Manheim. London: Eyre Methuen,
       1979, pb. (The threepenny opera).

1012   *Collected plays: Volume 5.* Ed. John Willett and
       Ralph Manheim. New York: Random/Pantheon Books,

BRECHT (cont'd).

1972. (Life of Galileo; Trial of Lucullus, Mother Courage).

1013 *Collected plays: Volume 6.* Ed. John Willett and Ralph Manheim. New York: Random/Vintage Books, 1976. (The good person of Szechwan; Puntila and Matti, his hired man; The resistable rise of Arturo Ui; Dansen; How much is your iron?; Practice pieces for actors).

1014 *Collected plays: Volume 7.* Ed. John Willett and Ralph Manheim. London: Eyre Methuen, 1976, pb; New York: Random House, n.d. (The visions of Simone Machard; Schweyk in the Second World War; The Caucasian chalk circle; The Duchess of Malfi).

1015 *Collected plays: Volume 9.* Ed. John Willett and Ralph Manheim. New York: Pantheon Books, 1972. (Adaptations: The tutor; Coriolanus; The trial of Joan of Arc at Rouen, 1431; Don Juan; Trumpets and drums).

1016 *Plays: Volume 1.* Trans. H.R. Hays, Eric Bentley and others. London: Methuen, 1960, 1965. (Caucasian chalk circle; Threepenny opera; Trial of Lucullus; Life of Galileo).

1017 *Plays: Volume 2.* Trans. Eric Bentley, Frank Jones and John Willett. London: Methuen, 1962, 1965. (Mother Courage and her children; St. Joan of the stockyards; The good person of Szechwan).

1018 *Poems.* Ed. John Willett and Ralph Manheim with the co-operation of Erich Fried. London: Eyre Methuen, 3 vols., 1976, pb; also in one-volume edition with index.

BRECHT (cont'd).

1019   *Seven plays.* Ed. and introd. Eric Bentley. New York: Grove Press, 1961. (In the swamp; A man's a man; St. Joan of the stockyards; Mother Courage; Galileo; The good woman of Setzuan; The Caucasian chalk circle).

1020   *Selected poems.* Bilingual. Trans. H.R. Hays. New York: Harcourt Brace, 1947, 1971, pb; London: Calder; New York: Grove Press, 1959, pb.

1021   *Brecht on theatre* (Kleines Organon für das Theater, et al). Ed. John Willett. London: Methuen; New York: Hill and Wang, 1964, pb.

1022   *Baal* (Baal). Trans. Eric Bentley and Martin Esslin. In Sokel, *Anthology of German expressionist drama.*

1023   *Baal. A man's a man. The elephant calf.* Trans. Eric Bentley. New York: Grove Press, 1964, pb.

1024   *Brecht's Hauspostille.* Bilingual. Trans. Sidney H. Bremer. Stanford: Stanford University Press, 1967. Cf. 1045.

1025   *The Caucasian chalk circle* (Die kaukasische Kreidekreis). Trans. Eric and Maja Bentley. London: Oxford University Press, 1956.

1026   *The Caucasian chalk circle.* Trans. Eric Bentley. New York: Grove Press, 1966; London, Glasgow: Blackie, 1967.

1027   *The Caucasian chalk circle.* Trans. Eric Bentley. In Bentley, *The great playwrights*, I.

BRECHT (cont'd).

1028   *The Caucasian chalk circle* (Der kaukasische Kreidekreis). Trans. Eric Bentley and Maja Apelman. In Corrigan, *Masterpieces of the modern German theatre.*

1029   *The Caucasian chalk circle.* Trans. Eric Bentley. In Corrigan, *The modern theatre.*

1030   *The Caucasian chalk circle.* Trans. Eric Bentley. In Esslin, *The genius of the German theater.*

1031   *The Caucasian chalk circle.* Trans. James and Tania Stern, with W.H. Auden. London: Methuen, 1963. Cf. 1056.

1032   *The days of the commune* (Die Tage der Kommune). Trans. Clive Barker and Arno Reinfrank. London: Methuen, 1978.

1033   *Edward the Second: A chronicle play* (Leben Eduards II. von England). Trans. Eric Bentley. New York: Grove Press, 1966, pb.

1034   *Galileo* (Leben des Galilei). Trans. Charles Laughton. Ed. Eric Bentley. New York: Grove Press, 1966, pb.

1035   *Galileo.* Trans. Charles Laughton. In Bentley, *From the modern repertoire*, II. Cf. 1044.

1036   *The good person of Szechwan* (Der gute Mensch von Setzuan). Trans. John Willett. London: Methuen, 1965, pb.

1037   *The good woman of Setzuan* (Der gute Mensch von Setzuan). Trans. Eric Bentley. New York: Grove Press, 1966, pb.

BRECHT (cont'd).

1038   *The good woman of Setzuan.* Trans. Eric Bentley.
In Block, *Masters of modern drama.*

1039   *The good woman of Setzuan.* Trans. Eric Bentley.
In Brockett, *Plays for the theatre.* Cf. 1056.

1040   *The great art of living together: Poems on the
theatre* (Messingkauf: extracts). Trans. John
Berger and Anna Bostock. Bingley: Granville
Press, 1972, pb. Cf. 1047.

1041   *The guns of Carrar* (Die Gewehre der Frau Carrar).
Trans. George Tabori. New York: S. French, 1971.

1042   *The Jewish wife, and other short plays.* Trans.
Eric Bentley. New York: Grove Press, 1965, pb.

1043   *The jungle of cities. Drums in the night. Round-
heads and Peakheads* (Im Dickicht der Städte.
Trommeln in der Nacht. Rundköpfe und Spitzköpfe).
Trans. Anselm Hollo, F. Jones, N. Goold-Verschoyle.
New York: Grove Press, 1966, pb.

1044   *The life of Galileo* (Leben des Galilei). Trans.
Desmond I. Vesey. London: Methuen, 1963, 1967.
Cf. 1034-35.

1045   *Manual of piety* (Hauspostille). Bilingual. Trans.
Eric Bentley. Ed. Hugo Schmidt. New York: Grove
Press, 1966, pb. Cf. 1024.

1046   *The measures taken* (Die Massnahme). In Bentley,
The modern theatre, VI.

1047   *The Messingkauf dialogues* (Der Messingkauf). Trans.
John Willett. London: Methuen, 1965. Cf. 1040.

BRECHT (cont'd).

1048   *Mr. Puntila and his man Matti* (Herr Puntila und
        sein Knecht Matti). Trans. John Willett. London:
        Eyre Methuen, 1977, pb.

1049   *The mother* (Die Mutter). Trans. Lee Baxandall.
        New York: Grove Press, 1965.

1050   *The mother*. Trans. Steve Gooch. London: Eyre
        Methuen, 1978.

1051   *Mother Courage and her children* (Mutter Courage
        und ihre Kinder). Trans. Eric Bentley. London:
        Methuen, 1962; New York: Grove Press, 1963, pb.

1052   *Mother courage*. Trans. Eric Bentley. In Bentley,
        The great playwrights, I.

1053   *Mother Courage*. Trans. Eric Bentley. In Block,
        Masters of modern drama.

1054   *Mother courage*. Trans. Eric Bentley. In Corrigan,
        The new theatre of Europe, II.

1055   *On Tao te Ching* (Zu Taoteking). Lexington, Ky.:
        Anvil, 1959.

1056   *Parables for the theatre: Two plays* (The good
        woman of Sezuan; The Caucasian chalk circle).
        Trans. Eric and Maja Bentley. London: Oxford
        University Press; Minneapolis: University of
        Minnesota Press, 1948, 1965; New York: Grove
        Press, 1957, pb. Cf. 1072.

1057   *Poems on the theatre*. Trans. John Berger and
        Anna Bostock. Northwood: Scorpion Press, 1961.

1058   *The private life of the master race* (Furcht und

125

BRECHT (cont'd).

Elend des dritten Reichs). Trans. Eric Bentley.
London: Gollancz, 1948.

1059 *The private life of the master race* (extract).
Trans. Eric Bentley. In Gassner, *A treasury of
the theatre*, II.

1060 *The resistable rise of Arturo Ui: A parable play*
(Der aufhaltsame Aufstieg des Arturo Ui). Trans.
Ralph Manheim. London: Eyre Methuen, 1976, pb.

1061 *The resistable rise of Arturo Ui.* Trans. and adapted by George Tabori. New York: S. French, 1972.

1062 *The rise and fall of the city of Mahagonny* (Aufstieg und Fall der Stadt Mahagonny). Trans. W.H.
Auden and Chester Kallman. Boston: D.R. Godine, 1976.

1063 *Saint Joan of the stockyards* (Die heilige Johanna
von den Schlachthöfen). Trans. Frank Jones.
Bloomington, Ind.: Indiana University Press, 1970,
pb; London: Eyre Methuen, 1976, pb.

1064 *Saint Joan of the stockyards.* Trans. Frank Jones.
In Bentley, *From the modern repertoire*, III.

1065 *Tales from the calendar* (Kalendergeschichten).
Trans. Yvonne Kapp and Michael Hamburger. London:
Methuen, 1961.

1066 *The threepenny novel* (Der Dreigroschenroman).
Trans. Demond I. Vesey. Verses by Christopher
Isherwood. London: 1937 (as *A penny for the poor*);
New York: Grove Press, 1956; London: Hanison, 1958;
Harmondsworth: Penguin, 1962, 1972, pb.

BRECHT (cont'd).

1067 *The threepenny opera* (Dreigroschenoper). Trans. Eric Bentley and Desmond Vesey. New York: Grove Press, 1964, pb.

1068 *The threepenny opera*. Trans. Eric Bentley and Desmond Vesey. In Bentley, *From the modern repertoire*, I.

1069 *The threepenny opera*. Trans. Eric Bentley and Desmond Vesey. In Bentley, *The modern theatre*, I.

1070 *The threepenny opera*. Trans. Desmond I. Vesey. Verses by Eric Bentley. In Esslin, *Three German plays*.

1071 *The threepenny opera*. Trans. Hugh MacDiarmid. London: Eyre Methuen, 1973.

1072 *Two plays: The good woman of Setzuan, and The Caucasian chalk circle*. Trans. Eric Bentley and Maja Apelman. New York: Grove Press, 1957; London: Calder, 1958. Previously published as *Parables for the theatre* (1948).

1073 *The visions of Simone Machard* (Die Gesichte der Simone Machard). Trans. Carl R. Mueller. New York: Grove Press, 1965, pb.

1074 *Diaries 1920-1922* (Tagebücher 1920-1922). Ed. Herta Ramthun. Trans. John Willett. London: Eyre Methuen, 1979.

1075 Selections in: Bridgwater, *Twentieth-century German verse*; Hamburger, *Modern German poetry*; Hamburger, *German poetry 1910-1975*; Hamburger, *East German poetry*; Kaufmann, *Twenty-five German poets*.

1076 BREDEL, Willi.

The death of General Moreau, and other stories.
Trans. Joan Becker. Berlin: Seven Seas Publ.,
1962.

1077 BREITBACH, Joseph.

Report on Bruno (Bericht über Bruno). Trans.
Michael Bullock. London: Panther, 1967.

1078 BRITTING, Georg.

The white slave trader (Der Mädchenhändler). Trans.
Geoffrey Skelton. In Yuill, German narrative prose,
II.

1079 BROCH, Hermann.

The atonement (Die Entsühnung). Trans. G.E. Wellwarth and H.F. Broch de Rothermann. In Wellwarth,
German drama between the wars.

1080 The unknown quantity: A novel (Die unbekannte
Grösse). Trans. Willa and Edwin Muir. London:
Collins, 1935; New York: Fertig, 1975.

1081 The death of Virgil (Der Tod des Vergil). Trans.
Jean Starr Untermeyer. New York: Pantheon, 1945;
New York: Grosset and Dunlap, 1965; Gloucester,
Mass.: P. Smith, 1966; London: Routledge and Kegan
Paul, 1946, 1977.

1082 The sleepwalkers: A trilogy (Die Schlafwandler).
Trans. W. and E. Muir. Introd. Hannah Arendt.
Boston, 1932; New York: Pantheon Books, 1947;
Grosset and Dunlap, 1964, pb.

1083 Zerline, the old servant girl. Trans. Jane B.
Greene. In Pick, German stories and tales.

1084 BROD, Max.

The master (Der Meister). Trans. H. Norden. New York: Philosophical Library, 1951.

1085 *The redemption of Tycho Brahe* (Tycho Brahes Weg zu Gott). Trans. F.W. Crosse. New York, 1928.

1086 *Unambo* (Unambo). Trans. L. Lewisohn. New York: Farrar, Straus, 1952.

1087 BRUCKNER, Ferdinand.

Elizabeth of England (Elisabeth von England). Trans. Ashley Dukes. London: Benn, 1931.

1088 *Races* (Die Rassen). Trans. Ruth Langner. New York, 1944.

1089 BRUST, Alfred.

The wolves (Die Wölfe). Trans. J.M. Ritchie. In Ritchie/Garten, *Seven expressionist plays.*

1090 BUBER, Martin.

For the sake of heaven (Gog und Magog). Trans. Ludwig Lewisohn. Philadelphia: Jewish Publication Society, 1945, 1959; New York: Harper, 1966; Westport, Conn.: Greenwood Press, 1970.

1091 *I and thou* (Ich und Du). Trans. Walter Kaufmann. Edinburgh: Clark, 1973, pb.

1092 *I and thou.* Trans. Ronald Gregor Smith. New York: Scribner, 1957; Edinburgh: Clark, 1959.

1093 *The legend of Baal-Shem* (Die Legende des Baalschem). Trans. Maurice Friedman. New York: Harper, 1955.

1094 *Tales of angels, spirits and demons.* Trans. David Antin and Jerome Rothenberg. New York: Hawk's Well, 1958.

BUBER (cont'd).

1095   *Tales of the Hasidim* (Die chassidischen Bücher).
        Trans. Olga Marx. New York: Schocken, 1947-48,
        2 vols.

1096   *Tales of Rabbi Nachman* (Die Geschichten des Rabbi
        Nachman). Trans. Maurice Friedman. New York:
        Horizon Press, 1956; New York: Avon Books, n.d.,
        pb; London: Souvenir Press, 1974, pb.

1097   *Ten rungs: Hasidic sayings.* Trans. Olga Marx.
        New York: Schocken, 1947.

1098 CANETTI, Elias.
        Auto da fé (Die Blendung). Trans. C.V. Wedgwood.
        London: Cape, 1946; New York: Stein and Day, 1964;
        New York: Avon Books, 1969, pb; Harmondsworth:
        Penguin, 1965, 1973, pb.

1099   *Crowds and power* (Masse und Macht). Trans. Carol
        Stewart. New York: The Seabury Press, 1978, pb.

1100   *The human province* (Die Provinz des Menschen).
        Trans. Joachim Neugroschel. New York: The Sea-
        bury Press, 1978.

1101   *The voices of Marrakesh: A record of a visit* (Die
        Stimmen von Marrakesch). Trans. J.A. Underwood.
        New York: The Seabury Press, 1978.

1102 CAROSSA, Hans.
        Doctor Gion (Der Arzt Gion). Trans. A.N. Scott.
        New York, London, 1933.

1103   *Year of sweet illusions* (Das Jahr der schönen
        Tauschungen). Trans. R. Kee. London: Methuen;
        New York: British Book Centre, 1951.

CAROSSA (cont'd).

1104   See also: Salinger, *Twentieth-century German verse*;
        Forster, *Penguin German verse.*

1105   CELAN, Paul.
        Nineteen poems. Trans. Michael Hamburger. Oxford:
        Carcanet Press, 1972.

1106   *Selected poems.* Trans. Michael Hamburger and
        Christopher Middleton. Harmondsworth: Penguin,
        1972, pb.

1107   *Speech-grille, and selected poems* (Sprachgitter).
        Bilingual. Trans. Joachim Neugroschel. New York:
        Dutton, 1971.

1108   See also: Rothenberg, *New young German poets*;
        Bridgwater, *Twentieth-century German verse*;
        Hamburger, *Modern German poetry*; Hamburger, *German
        poetry 1910-1975*; Schwebell, *Contemporary German
        poetry.*

1109   CHLUMBERG, Hans.
        Miracle at Verdun (Wunder um Verdun). Trans.
        Edward Crankshaw. London: Gollancz, 1932.

1110   *Miracle at Verdun* (Wunder um Verdun). Trans.
        Julian Leigh. New York: Brentano, 1931.

1111   CIBULKA, Hanns.
        Selections in: Deicke, *Time for dreams.*

1112   DAUTHENDEY, Max.
        Selections in: Deutsch, *Contemporary German poetry*;
        Bithell, *Contemporary German poetry.*

1113   DEHMEL, Richard.
        Selections in: Deutsch, *Contemporary German poetry*;

DEHMEL (cont'd).

Bithell, *Contemporary German poetry*; Francke, *The German classics*, XVIII.

1114 DEICKE, Günther.

Selections in: Deicke, *Time for dreams*.

1115 DODERER, Heimito von.

The demons (Die Dämonen). Trans. Richard and Clara Winston. New York: Knopf, 1961, 2 vols.

1116 *Every man a murderer* (Ein Mord, den jeder begeht). Trans. Richard and Clara Winston. New York: Knopf, 1964.

1117 *The waterfalls of Slunj* (Die Wasserfälle von Slunj). Trans. Eithne Wilkins and Ernst Kaiser. New York: Harcourt, Brace and World, 1966.

1118 DÖBLIN, Alfred.

Alexanderplatz Berlin: The story of Franz Biber-kopf (Berlin Alexanderplatz). Trans. Eugene Jolas. New York: Viking; London: Secker, 1931; New York: Ungar, 1958, pb; London: Secker and Warburg, 1974.

1119 *Men without mercy* (Pardon wird nicht gegeben). Trans. Trevor and Phyllis Blewitt. London: Gollancz, 1937; New York: Howard Fertig, 1976.

1120 DORST, Tankred.

Three plays. Trans. (adapted) Henry Beissel. Toronto: Playwrights Co-op, 1976.

1121 *The curve* (Die Kurve). Trans. James L. Rosenberg. In Corrigan, *The new theatre of Europe*, III.

1122 *Freedom for Clemens* (Freiheit für Clemens). Trans. George E. Wellwarth. In Benedikt/Wellwarth, *Post-war German theatre*.

1123 DÜRRENMATT, Friedrich.

Four plays, 1957-1962. Various translators.
London: Cape, 1964; New York: Grove Press, 1965.
(Romulus the great; The marriage of Mr. Mississippi;
An angel comes to Babylon; The physicists. Also
contains the essay "Problems of the theatre").

1124 An angel comes to Babylon. Romulus the great
(Ein Engel kommt nach Babylon. Romulus der Grosse).
Trans. William McElwee and Gerhard Nellhaus. New
York: Grove Press, 1964, pb.

1125 A dangerous game (Die Panne). Trans. Richard and
Clara Winston. London: Cape, 1960. Cf. 1138.

1126 Incident at twilight (Abendstunde im Spätherbst).
Trans. George E. Wellwarth. In Benedikt/Wellwarth,
Postwar German theatre.

1127 Incident at twilight. Trans. G.E. Wellwarth. In
Wellwarth, Themes of drama.

1128 The judge and his hangman (Der Richter und sein
Henker). Trans. Cyrus Brooks. London: Jenkins,
1954; London: Four Square Press, 1961, pb; London:
Cape, 1967; Harmondsworth: Penguin, 1969, pb.

1129 The judge and his hangman. Trans. Therese Pol.
New York: Harper and Row, 1955; New York: Berkeley,
1958, pb; New York: Doubleday, 1963, pb.

1130 The marriage of Mr. Mississippi: A play (Die Ehe
des Herrn Mississippi). Trans. Michael Bullock.
New York: Grove Press, 1966, pb. Cf. 1136.

1131 The meteor (Der Meteor). Trans. James Kirkup.
London: Cape, 1973, pb.

DÜRRENMATT (cont'd).

1132   *Once a Greek* (Grieche sucht Griechin). Trans.
        Richard and Clara Winston. New York: Knopf,
        1965; London: Cape, 1966.

1133   *The physicists* (Die Physiker). Trans. James
        Kirkup. London: French, 1963; New York: Grove
        Press, 1964, pb; London: Cape, 1973, pb.

1134   *Play Strindberg* (Play Strindberg). Trans. James
        Kirkup. London: Cape, 1972; New York: Grove
        Press, 1973.

1135   *The pledge* (Das Versprechen). Trans. Richard and
        Clara Winston. London: Cape; New York: Knopf,
        1959; New York: New American Library, 1960, pb;
        Harmondsworth: Penguin, 1964, pb.

1136   *Problems of the theatre. The marriage of Mr.
        Mississippi* (Theaterprobleme. Die Ehe des Herrn
        Mississippi). Trans. Gerhard Nellhaus, Michael
        Bullock. New York: Grove Press, 1964.

1137   *The quarry* (Der Verdacht). Trans. Eva H. Morreale.
        Greenwich, Conn.: New York Graphic Society; London:
        Cape; New York: Grove Press, 1962, pb.

1138   *Traps* (Die Panne). Trans. Richard and Clara
        Winston. New York: Knopf, 1960, pb; New York:
        Ballantine, 1965, pb. Cf. 1125.

1139   *The visit* (Der Besuch der alten Dame). Trans.
        Patrick Bowles. London: Cape; New York: Grove
        Press, 1962, 1973, pb.

1140   *The visit.* Trans. Patrick Bowles. In Corrigan,
        The modern theatre.

DÜRRENMATT (cont'd).

1141   *The visit*. Adapted by Maurice Valency. New
       York: Random House, 1958; New York: French, 1960,
       pb.

1142   *The visit*. Trans. Maurice Valency. In Block,
       Masters of modern drama.

1143 EDSCHMID, Kasimir.
       The humiliating room. Trans. R.P. Heller, In
       Yuill, *German narrative prose*, II.

1144 EICH, Günter.
       Darmstadt address (Darmstädter Rede). Trans.
       Michael Hamburger. In Middleton, *German writing
       today*.

1145   *Poems*. Bilingual. Trans. Teo Savory. Santa
       Barbara: Unicorn Press, 1971, pb.

1146   *Journeys: Two radio plays* (Die Brandung vor
       Setubal; Das Jahr Lacertis). Trans. Michael
       Hamburger. London: Cape; New York: Grossmann,
       1968, pb.

1147   Selections in: Hamburger, *German poetry 1910-
       1975*; Schwebell, *Contemporary German poetry*.

1148 EINSTEIN, Albert.
       Ideas and opinions (Mein Weltbild). Ed. Carl
       Seelig. Trans. Sonja Bergmann. New York: Crown,
       1954.

1149 ELSNER, Gisela.
       The giant dwarfs (Die Riesenzwerge). Trans. Joel
       Carmichael. London: Weidenfeld and Nicolson; New
       York: Grove Press, 1965.

1150　ENDLER, Adolf.
Selections in: Deicke, *Time for dreams*.

1151　ENZENSBERGER, Christian.
Smut: An anatomy of dirt (Grösserer Versuch über
den Schmutz). Trans. Sandra Morris. London:
Calder and Boyars, 1972.

1152　ENZENSBERGER, Hans Magnus.
The Havana inquiry (Das Verhör von Habana). Trans.
Peter Mayer. New York: Holt Rinehart and Winston,
1974.

1153　*Poems*. Bilingual. Trans. Michael Hamburger,
Jerome Rothenberg, and the author. London:
Secker and Warburg; New York: Atheneum; Harmonds-
worth: Penguin, 1968, pb.

1154　*Poems*. Trans. Michael Hamburger. Newcastle-on-
Tyne: Northern House, 1966.

1155　*Politics and crime*. Selected by Michael Roloff.
New York: Seabury Press, 1974.

1156　See also: Rothenberg, *New young German poets*;
Hamburger, *German poetry 1910-1975*; Schwebell,
Contemporary German poetry.

1157　ERNST, Otto.
Master Flachsmann (Flachsmann als Erzieher).
Trans. H.M. Beatty. London: Unwin, 1909; New
York: Duffield, 1912.

1158　FALLADA, Hans (Rudolf Ditzen).
The drinker (Der Trinker). Trans. C. and A.
Lloyd. London: Putnam; New York: Didier, 1952;
Dell, 1956.

FALLADA (cont'd).

1159   *Iron Gustav* (Der eiserne Gustav). Trans. Philip
        Owens. London: Putnam, 1940; London: Howard
        Baker, 1969.

1160   *Little man, what now?* (Kleiner Mann, was nun?).
        Trans. Eric Sutton. New York: Simon and Schuster,
        1933; New York: Ungar, 1957, pb. London: Howard
        Baker, 1969.

1161   *That rascal, Fridolin* (Fridolin, der freche Dachs).
        Trans. Ruth Michaelis-Jena and Arthur Ratcliff.
        London: Heinemann; New York: Pantheon Books, 1959.

1162   *Who once eats out of the tin bowl* (Wer einmal aus
        dem Blechnapf frisst). Trans. Eric Sutton. Lon-
        don: Putnam, 1934; London: Howard Baker, 1969.

1163   *Wolf among wolves* (Wolf unter Wölfen). Trans.
        Philip Owens. New York, London: Putnam, 1938;
        London: Howard Baker, 1970.

1164   FASSBINDER, Rainer Werner.
        Bremen coffee. Trans. Anthony Vivis. In: Wolf-
        gang Bauer, *Shakespeare the sadist* (London: Eyre
        Methuen, 1977, pb).

1165   FEUCHTWANGER, Lion.
        House of Desdemona. Trans. Harold A. Basilius.
        Detroit, Mich.: Wayne State University Press,
        1963, pb.

1166   *Jephthah and his daughter* (Jefta und seine Tochter).
        Trans. Eithne Wilkins and Ernst Kaiser. London:
        Hutchinson; New York: Putnam, 1958; New York:
        New American Library, 1960, pb.

FEUCHTWANGER (cont'd).

1167   *Jew Süss* (Jud Süss). Trans. W. and E. Muir.
       London: Secker, 1926; New York: Viking Press,
       1948; New York: Avon Press, 1951, pb (American
       edn.: *Power*).

1168   *Josephus: A historical romance* (Der jüdische
       Krieg). New York: Atheneum, 1972, pb.

1169   *Marianne in India, and other stories* (Marianne
       in Indien). New York: Avon, 1948.

1170   *Odysseus and the swine, and other stories.* London:
       Hutchinson, 1949.

1171   *The Oppermanns* (Die Geschwister Oppenheim). New
       York: Universal Publishers, 1964, pb.

1172   *Proud destiny* (Waffen für Amerika). Trans. Moray
       Firth. New York: Viking, 1947; New York: Garden
       City, 1949; New York: Doubleday, 1949; London:
       Hutchinson, 1952; New York: Popular Library, n.d.,
       pb.

1173   *Raquel, the Jewess of Toledo* (Die Jüdin von Toledo).
       Trans. Eithne Wilkins and Ernst Kaiser. London:
       Hutchinson; New York: Messner, 1956; New York:
       New American Library, 1957, pb; New York: Signet,
       1960.

1174   *Simone* (Simone). Trans. G.A. Herman. New York:
       Garden City, 1946.

1175   *Stories from far and near.* New York: Viking, 1945.

1176   *This is the hour* (Goya, oder Der arge Weg zur
       Erkenntnis). Trans. Helen Tracy Lowe-Porter and
       F. Fawcett. New York: Viking Press, 1951; London:

FEUCHTWANGER (cont'd).

Hutchinson, 1952, 1956; New York: Heritage Press, 1956; New York: Popular Library, 1964, pb.

1177 *'Tis folly to be wise* (Narrenweisheit). Trans. F. Fawcett. New York: Messner, 1953; London: Hutchinson, 1954.

1178 *Ugly Duchess* (Die hässliche Herzogin Margaret Maultasch). Trans. W. and E. Muir. London: Secker, 1927; New York: Avon Press, 1957, pb; London: Hutchinson, 1972.

1179 *The widow Capet* (Die Witwe Capet). Los Angeles: Pacific Press, 1956.

1180 *The visions of Simone Machard* (Die Gesichte der Simone Machard). Trans. Carl R. Mueller. New York: Grove Press, 1965, pb.

1181 FRANK, Bruno.
The days of the king (Tage des Königs). Trans. H.T. Lowe-Porter. Freeport, N.Y.: Books for Libraries Press, 1970.

1182 *Twelve thousand* (Zwölftausend). Trans. W.A. Drake. New York: Knopf; London: Allen, 1928

1183 FRANK, Leonhard.
The baroness. Trans. C. Brooks. London: Nevill, 1950.

1184 *Beloved stranger.* Trans. Cyrus Brooks. New York: Garden City, 1947.

1185 *Desire me, and other stories.* Trans. C. Brooks. New York: Garden City, 1957; New York: New American Library, 1957, pb; Baltimore, Penguin, 1948.

FRANK, Leonhard (cont'd).

1186   *Dream mates* (Die Traumgefährten). Trans. Maxim
Newmark. New York: Philosophical Library, 1946.

1187   *Heart on the left* (Links wo das Herz ist). Trans.
C. Brooks. London: Barker, 1954.

1188   *Karl and Anna* (Karl und Anna). Trans. R. Langner.
New York, 1929.

1189   *Karl and Anna.* Trans. L.W. Lockhart. London, 1930.

1190   *Mathilde* (Mathilde). Trans. W.R. Trask. New
York: Simon and Schuster; London P. Davies, 1948.

1191 FRENSSEN, Gustav.
Holyland (Hilligenlei). Trans. M.A. Hamilton.
London and Boston, 1906.

1192   *Jörn Uhl* (Jörn Uhl). Trans. F.S. Delmer. London,
Boston, 1905; New York, 1913, 1922.

1193   *The life of Jesus.* Trans. M.A. Hamilton. In
Francke, *The German classics,* XVII.

1194   *Otto Babendiek* (Otto Babendiek). Trans. Huntley
Paterson. London: Harrap, 1930, 1932.

1195 FREUD, Sigmund.
Works. Ed. James Strachey. Trans. various.
London: Hogarth Press, 1953-   , 24 vols.

1196 FRIED, Erich.
Last honours. Bilingual. Trans. Georg Rapp.
London: Turret, 1968 (lim. ed.).

1197   *On pain of seeing: Poems.* Sel. and trans. Georg
Rapp. London: Rapp and Whiting; Chicago: Swallow
Press, 1969.

1198 FRISCH, Max.
*Four plays: The great wall of China. Don Juan.
Philipp Hotz's fury. Biography.* Trans. Michael
Bullock. London: Methuen, 1969.

1199 *Three plays: Don Juan. The great rage of Phillip
Hotz. When the war was over.* Trans. James L.
Rosenberg. New York: Hill and Wang, 1967, pb.

1200 *Three plays: The fire raisers. Count Oederland.
Andorra.* Trans. Michael Bullock. London: Methuen,
1962.

1201 *Andorra* (Andorra). Trans. Michael Bullock. New
York: Hill and Wang, 1964, pb.

1202 *Biedermann and the firebugs* (Biedermann und die
Brandstifter). Trans. Mordecai Gorelik. In
Block, *Masters of modern drama.* Cf. 1206.

1203 *Biography: A game* (Biografie). Trans. Michael
Bullock. New York: Hill and Wang, 1969.

1204 *The Chinese wall* (Die chinesische Mauer). Trans.
James L. Rosenberg. New York: Hill and Wang,
1961, pb.

1205 *The chinese wall.* Trans. James L. Rosenberg. In
Corrigan, *The modern theatre.*

1206 *The firebugs* (Biedermann und die Brandstifter).
Trans. Mordecai Gorelik. New York: Hill and Wang,
1963, pb. Cf. 1202.

1207 *The great fury of Philip Hotz* (Die grosse Wut des
Philipp Hotz). Trans. Michael Benedikt. In
Benedikt/Wellwarth, *Postwar German theatre.*

FRISCH (cont'd).

1208 *Homo Faber: A report* (Homo Faber). Trans. Michael Bullock. London, New York: Abelard-Schuman, 1959; New York: Harcourt Brace Jovanovich, 1971, pb; Harmondsworth: Penguin, 1974, pb.

1209 *I'm not Stiller* (Stiller). Trans. Michael Bullock. London, New York: Abelard-Schuman, 1958; Harmondsworth: Penguin, 1961, pb; New York: Random House, 1962, pb.

1210 *Montauk* (Montauk). Trans. Geoffrey Skelton. New York: Harcourt Brace Jovanovich, 1976.

1211 *Now they sing again* (Nun singen sie wieder). Trans. David Lommen. See Roloff, *The contemporary German theater.*

1212 *A wilderness of mirrors* (Mein Name sei Gantenbein). Trans. Michael Bullock. London: Methuen, 1965, 1967, pb; New York: Random, 1966.

1213 *Sketchbook, 1946-1949* (Tagebuch 1946-1949). Trans. Geoffrey Skelton. New York, London: Harcourt Brace Jovanovich, 1977.

1214 *Sketchbook, 1966-1971* (Tagebuch, 1966-1971). Trans. Geoffrey Skelton. New York: Harcourt Brace Jovanovich, 1974; London: Eyre Methuen, 1974.

1215 FÜHMANN, Franz.

  Selections in: Deicke, *Time for dreams.*

1216 FUSSENEGGER, Gertrud.

  See: Newnham, *German short stories.*

1217 GAISER, Gerd.

The falling leaf (Die sterbende Jagd). Trans.
Paul Findlay. London: Collins, 1956. Cf. 1221.

1218 The final ball (Schlussball). Trans. Marguerite
Waldman. New York: Pantheon Books, 1960. Cf.1220.

1219 The game of murder. Trans. H.M. Waidson. In
Spender, Great German short stories.

1220 The last dance of the season (Schlussball). Trans.
Marguerite Waldman. London: Collins, 1960. Cf.1218.

1221 The last squadron (Die sterbende Jagd). Trans.
Paul Findlay. New York: Pantheon Books, 1956;
London: Collins, 1960, pb. Cf. 1217

1222 See also: Newnham, German short stories; Lamport,
German short stories.

1223 GEORGE, Stefan.

The works of Stefan George. Trans. Olga Marx and
Ernst Morwitz. Chapel Hill, N.C.: University of
North Carolina Press, 1949, 1974.

1224 Poems. Bilingual. Trans. Carol North Valhope
and Ernst Morwitz. New York: Schocken, 1967, pb.

1225 See also: Flores, Anthology of German poetry;
Francke, The German classics, XVIII; Salinger,
Twentieth century German verse; Forster, Penguin
German verse; Kaufmann, Twenty-five German poets;
Deutsch, Contemporary German poetry.

1226 GERLACH, Jens.

Selections in: Deicke, Time for dreams.

1227   GOERING, Reinhard.
       Naval encounter (Seeschlacht). Trans. J.M. Ritchie
       and J.D. Stowell. In Ritchie, *Vision and aftermath*.

1228   GOES, Albrecht.
       Arrow to the heart (Unruhige Nacht). Trans. C.
       Fitzgibbon. London: Joseph, 1951. Cf. 1230.

1229   *The burnt offering* (Das Brandopfer). Trans.
       Michael Hamburger. London: Gollancz; New York:
       Pantheon Books, 1956.

1230   *Unquiet night* (Unruhige Nacht). Trans. C. Fitz-
       gibbon. Boston: Houghton Mifflin, 1951. Cf. 1228.

1231   GOLL, Ivan.
       The immortal one (Die Unsterblichen). Trans.
       Walter H. and Jacqueline Sokel. In Sokel, *Antho-
       logy of German expressionist'drama*.

1232   *Methusalem* (Methusalem). Trans. J.M. Ritchie.
       In Ritchie/Garten, *Seven expressionist plays*.

1233   Selections in: Hamburger, *Modern German poetry*.

1234   GOMRINGER, Eugen.
       The book of hours: Constellations. Trans. Jerome
       Rothenberg. New York: Something Else Press, 1968.

1235   GONG, Alfred.
       Selections in: Schwebell, *Contemporary German
       poetry*.

1236   GRAF, Oskar Maria.
       Old-fashioned poems of an ordinary man (Altmodische
       Gedichte eines Dutzendmenschen). Trans. Elisabeth
       Bayliss. New York: Herald Press, 1967.

1237 GRAF (cont'd).

Prisoners all (Wir sind Gefangene). Trans. Margaret Green. New York: Knopf, 1928.

1238 GRASS, Günter.

Four plays: Flood, Mister Mister, Only ten minutes to Buffalo, The wicked cooks. Trans. Ralph Manheim and A. Leslie Willson. Ed. Martin Esslin. London: Secker and Warburg; New York: Harcourt Brace Jovanovich, 1967, pb; Harmondsworth: Penguin, 1972, pb.

1239 *New poems* (Ausgefragt). Bilingual. Trans. Michael Hamburger. New York: Harcourt, Brace and World, 1968.

1240 *Poems of Günter Grass.* Trans. Michael Hamburger and Christopher Middleton. Harmondsworth: Penguin, 1969, pb.

1241 *Selected poems.* Bilingual. Trans. Michael Hamburger and Christopher Middleton. New York: Harcourt, Brace and World, 1966; London: Secker and Warburg, 1966.

1242 *Cat and mouse* (Katz und Maus). Trans. Ralph Manheim. New York: Harcourt, Brace and World; London: Secker and Warburg, 1963; New York: New American Library (Signet), 1964, pb; Harmondsworth: Penguin, 1966, pb.

1243 *Dog years* (Hundejahre). Trans. Ralph Manheim. London: Secker and Warburg, 1965; New York: Harcourt, Brace and World, 1965; Greenwich, Conn.: Fawcett, 1966, 1969, pb; Harmondsworth: Penguin, 1969, pb.

GRASS (cont'd).

1244   *The flounder* (Der Butt). Trans. Ralph Manheim.
New York: Harcourt Brace Jovanovich, 1978; New
York: Fawcett Crest, 1979, pb.

1245   *From the diary of a snail* (Aus dem Tagebuch einer
Schnecke). Trans. Ralph Manheim. New York: Harcourt Brace Jovanovich, 1973, 1976; London: Secker
and Warburg, 1974; Harmondsworth: Penguin, 1976, pb.

1246   *Inmarypraise* (Mariazuehren). Trans. Christopher
Middleton. New York: Harcourt Brace Jovanovich,
1974.

1247   *In the egg, and other poems.* Bilingual. Trans.
Michael Hamburger and Christopher Middleton. New
York: Harcourt Brace Jovanovich, 1977, pb.

1248   *Local anaesthetic* (Örtlich betäubt). Trans.
Ralph Manheim. New York: Harcourt, Brace and
World; London: Secker and Warburg, 1969; Har-
mondsworth: Penguin, 1973, pb.

1249   *Love tested* (Liebe geprüft). Trans. Michael
Hamburger. New York: Harcourt Brace Jovanovich,
1975.

1250   *Max: A play* (Davor). Trans. A. Leslie Willson
and Ralph Manheim. New York: Harcourt Brace
Jovanovich, 1972, pb.

1251   *The plebeians rehearse the uprising* (Die Plebejer
proben den Aufstand). Trans. Ralph Manheim. New
York: Harcourt, Brace and World, 1966, pb; London:
Secker and Warburg, 1967; Harmondsworth: Penguin,
1972, pb.

GRASS (cont'd).

1252 *Rocking back and forth* (Beritten hin und zurück).
Trans. Michael Benedikt and Joseph Goradza. In
Benedikt/Wellwarth, *Postwar German theatre.*

1253 *The Salt Lake line* (Noch zehn Minuten bis Buffalo).
Trans. Christopher Holme. In Middleton, *German
writing today.*

1254 *Speak out: Speeches, open letters, commentaries*
(Über das Selbstverständliche). Trans. Ralph
Manheim. London: Secker and Warburg; New York:
Harcourt, Brace and World, 1969, pb.

1255 *The tin drum* (Die Blechtrommel). Trans. Ralph
Manheim. London: Secker and Warburg, 1961; New
York: Random, 1964, pb; New York: Fawcett, 1964;
Harmondsworth: Penguin, 1965, pb.

1256 *The wicked cooks* (Die bösen Köche). Trans. James
L. Rosenberg. In Corrigan, *The new theatre of
Europe*, II.

1257 See also: Rothenberg, *New young German poets*;
Hamburger, *German poetry 1910-1975.*

1258 GÜTERSLOH, Albert Paris von.
The fraud: A novel (Der Lügner unter Bürgern).
Trans. John Nowell. London: Owen, 1965.

1259 HAGELSTANGE, Rudolf.
Ballad of the buried life (Ballade vom verschütteten
Leben). Bilingual. Trans. Herman Salinger. Chapel Hill, N.C.: University of North Carolina Press,
1962, pb.

1260 HANDKE, Peter.
The goalie's anxiety at the penalty kick (Die Angst
des Tormanns beim Elfmeter). Trans. Michael Roloff.
New York: Farrar, Straus and Giroux, 1972; London:
Eyre Methuen, 1977.

1261 *The innerworld of the outerworld of the innerworld*
(Die Innenwelt der Aussenwelt der Innenwelt). Bi-
lingual. Trans. Michael Roloff. New York: Seabury
Press, 1974.

1262 *Kaspar* (Kaspar). Trans. Michael Roloff. London:
Eyre Methuen, 1972, pb.

1263 *Kaspar, and other plays*. Trans. Michael Roloff.
New York: Farrar, Straus and Giroux, 1969.

1264 *The left-handed woman* (Die linkshändige Frau).
Trans. Ralph Manheim. New York: Farrar, Straus
and Giroux, 1978.

1265 *A moment of true feeling* (Die Stunde der wahren
Empfindung). Trans. Ralph Manheim. New York:
Farrar, Straus and Giroux, 1977.

1266 *My foot my tutor* (Das Mündel will Vormund sein).
Trans. Michael Roloff. In Wolfgang Bauer, *Shakespeare the sadist* (London: Eyre Methuen, 1977, pb).

1267 *Nonsense and happiness* (Als das Wünschen noch
geholfen hat). Trans. Michael Roloff. New York:
Urizen books, 1976, pb.

1268 *Offending the audience. Self accusation* (Publi-
kumsbeschimpfung. Selbstbezichtigung). Trans.
Michael Roloff. New York: Farrar, Straus and
Giroux, 1969; London: Methuen, 1971, pb. Cf. 1271.

HANDKE (cont'd).

1269　*The ride across Lake Constance* (Der Ritt über
den Bodensee). Trans. Michael Roloff. London:
Eyre Methuen, 1973, pb.

1270　*The ride across Lake Constance* (Der Ritt über den
Bodensee). Trans. Michael Roloff. In Roloff,
The contemporary German theatre.

1271　*Self-accusation* (Selbstbezichtigung). Trans.
Michael Roloff. In Corrigan/Esslin, *The new
theatre of Europe*, IV.

1272　*Short letter, long farewell* (Der kurze Brief zum
langen Abschied). Trans. Ralph Manheim. New
York: Farrar, Straus and Giroux, 1974; London:
Eyre Methuen, 1977.

1273　*A sorrow beyond dreams: A life story* (Wunschloses
Unglück). Trans. Ralph Manheim. New York:
Farrar, Straus and Giroux, 1975; London: Souvenir
Press, 1976, pb.

1274　*They are dying out* (Die Unvernünftigen sterben
aus). Trans. Michael Roloff, in collaboration
with Karl Weber. London: Eyre Methuen, 1975, pb.

1274a　*Three by Peter Handke*. Trans. Ralph Manheim and
Michael Roloff. New York: Bard/Avon, 1977, pb.
(The goalie's anxiety at the penalty kick; Short
letter, long farewell; A sorrow beyond dreams).

1275　Selections in: Hamburger, *German poetry 1910-1975*.

1276　HARDT, Ernst.
Tantris the fool (Tantris der Narr). Trans. W.
Noble and J. James. St. Louis, 1909.

HARDT (cont'd).

1277   *Tristram the jester* (Tantris der Narr). Trans.
        John Heard. In Francke, *The German classics*, XX.

1278 HASENCLEVER, Walter.
        Antigone (Antigone). Trans. J.M. Ritchie. In
        Ritchie, *Vision and aftermath*.

1279   and Kurt Tucholsky. *Christopher Columbus* (Chris-
        toph Columbus). Trans. Max Spalter and G.E. Well-
        warth. In Wellwarth, *German drama between the
        wars*.

1280   *Humanity* (Die Menschen). Trans. Walter H. and
        Jacqueline Sokel. In Sokel, *Anthology of German
        expressionist drama*.

1281 HAUPTMANN, Carl.
        War, a Te Deum (Krieg, ein Tedeum). Trans. J.M.
        Ritchie. In Ritchie, *Vision and aftermath*.

1282 HEISENBÜTTEL, Helmut.
        Texts. Sel. and trans. Michael Hamburger. London:
        Calder and Boyars, 1977, pb.

1283   Selections in: Rothenberg, *New young German poets*;
        Hamburger, *German poetry 1910-1975*.

1284 HERBURGER, Günter.
        A monotonous landscape: Seven stories (Eine
        gleichmässige Landschaft). Trans. Geoffrey
        Skelton. New York: Harcourt, Brace and World,
        1968; London: Calder and Boyars, 1969.

1285 HERMLIN, Stephan.
        City on a hill: A quartet in prose. Trans. Joan
        Becker. Berlin: Seven Seas Publ.; London: Collet,
        1962.

1286   HESSE, Hermann.

      Poems. Bilingual. Trans. James Wright. New
      York: Farrar, Straus and Giroux, 1970, pb; London:
      Cape, 1971, 1977, pb.

1287   *Stories of five decades.* Ed. Theodore Ziolkowski.
      Trans. Ralph Manheim and Denver Lindley. New
      York: Farrar, Straus and Giroux, 1972; London:
      Cape, 1974; St. Albans: Triad/Panther, 1976, pb.

1288   *Beneath the wheel* (Unterm Rad). Trans. Michael
      Roloff. New York: Farrar, Straus and Giroux, 1968,
      1972, pb. New York: Bantam, 1970, pb. Cf. 1310.

1289   *Crisis: Pages from a diary* (Krisis, ein Stück
      Tagebuch). Bilingual. Trans. Ralph Manheim.
      New York: Farrar, Straus and Giroux, 1975.

1290   *Death and the lover* (Narziss und Goldmund). Trans.
      Geoffrey Dunlop. London: Jarrolds, 1932; New York:
      Ungar, 1959. Cf. 1296, 1306-07.

1291   *Demian* (Demian). Trans. N.H. Priday. New York:
      Boni and Liveright, 1923; Henry Holt, 1948.

1292   *Demian.* Trans. Michael Roloff and Michael Lebeck.
      New York: Harper and Row, 1965; New York: Bantam,
      1966, 1970.

1293   *Demian.* Trans. Walter J. Strachan. London: Owen,
      1958; London: Panther, 1969, pb.

1294   *Gertrude* (Gertrud). Trans. Hilda Rosner. London:
      Owen, 1955, 1963; Hollywood, Fla.: Transatlantic
      Arts, 1956; New York: Farrar, Straus and Giroux,
      1969, pb; Harmondsworth: Penguin, 1973, pb; New
      York: Bantam, 1974, pb.

HESSE (cont'd).

1295   *The glass bead game* (Das Glasperlenspiel). Trans.
        Richard and Clara Winston. New York: Holt, Rine-
        hart and Winston, 1969; London: Cape, 1970; Har-
        mondsworth: Penguin, 1972, pb. Cf. 1303-04.

1296   *Goldmund* (Narziss und Goldmund). Trans. Geoffrey
        Dunlop. London: P. Owen/Vision Press, 1959, 1968;
        Chester Springs, Pa.: Dufour, 1959; originally
        published as *Death and the lover* (1932). Cf. 1290,
        1306-07

1297   *Hours in the garden, and other poems.* Trans. Rika
        Lesser. New York: Farrar, Straus and Giroux, 1978,
        pb.

1298   *If the war goes on* (Krieg und Frieden). Trans.
        Ralph Manheim. New York: Farrar, Straus and
        Giroux, 1971, 1973, pb; London: Cape, 1972;
        London: Pan Books, 1974, pb.

1299   *In the old 'Sun.'* Trans. A. Coleman. In Francke,
        The German classics, XIX.

1300   *The journey to the East* (Die Morgenlandfahrt).
        Trans. Hilda Rosner. London: P. Owen/Vision Press,
        1956, 1970; New York: Noonday Press, 1957, pb; New
        York: Farrar, Straus and Giroux, 1968, 1973, pb;
        St. Albans: Panther Books, 1972, pb; New York:
        Bantam, 1972, pb; London: Pan Books, 1974, pb.

1301   *Klingsor's last summer* (Klingsors letzter Sommer).
        Trans. Richard and Clara Winston. New York: Farrar,
        Straus and Giroux, 1970, pb; London: Cape, 1971;
        London: Pan Books, 1973, pb; New York: Bantam, 1974,
        pb.

HESSE (cont'd).

1302   *Knulp: Three tales from the life of Knulp* (Knulp).
Trans. Ralph Manheim. New York: Farrar, Straus
and Giroux, 1971, 1973, pb; London: Cape, 1972;
London: Pan Books, 1974, pb.

1303   *Magister Ludi* (Das Glasperlenspiel). Trans.
Mervyn Savill. New York: Holt, 1949, 1968;
London: Aldus Publ., 1950; New York: Ungar, 1957,
1965.

1304   *Magister Ludi (The glass bead game)*. Trans.
Richard and Clara Winston. Introd. Theodore
Ziolkowski. New York: Bantam, 1969, 1973, pb.
Cf. 1295.

1305   *My belief: Essays on life and art* (Mein Glauben).
Ed. Theodore Ziolkowski. Trans. Denver Lindley
and Ralph Manheim. New York: Farrar, Straus and
Giroux, 1974; London: Cape, 1976.

1306   *Narcissus and Goldmund* (Narziss und Golmund).
Trans. Ursule Molinaro. New York: Farrar, Straus
and Giroux, 1968, 1972, pb; New York: Bantam,
1971, pb.

1307   *Narziss and Goldmund*. Trans. Geoffrey Dunlop.
Harmondsworth: Penguin, 1971, pb. Originally
published as *Death and the lover* (1932), then
as *Goldmund* (1959). Cf. 1290, 1296.

1308   *Peter Camenzind* (Peter Camenzind). Trans. Michael
Roloff. New York: Farrar, Straus and Giroux,
1969, 1973, pb.

HESSE (cont'd).

1309   *Peter Camenzind*. Trans. Walter J. Strachan.
        London: Owen/Vision Press, 1961, 1968; Harmonds-
        worth: Penguin, 1973, pb.

1310   *The prodigy* (Unterm Rad). Trans. Walter J. Stra-
        chan. London: Owen/Vision Press, 1957, 1968;
        Calcutta: Rupa, 1961; Harmondsworth: Penguin,
        1973, pb. Cf. 1288.

1311   *Reflections* (Lektüre fur Minuten). Trans. Ralph
        Manheim. New York: Farrar, Straus and Giroux, 1974.

1312   *Rosshalde* (Rosshalde). Trans. Ralph Manheim.
        New York: Farrar, Straus and Giroux, 1970, pb;
        New York: Bantam, 1971, pb: London: Cape, 1971;
        London: Pan Books, 1972, 1974.

1313   *Siddhartha* (Siddhartha). Trans. Hilda Rosner.
        New York: New Directions, 1951, 1974; London:
        Owen/Vision Press, 1954, 1970; New York: Ungar,
        1957; Calcutta: Rupa, 1958; New York: Bantam,
        1971, 1974; London Pan Books, 1974, pb.

1314   *Steppenwolf* (Steppenwolf). Trans. Basil Creighton.
        London: Secker; New York: Holt, 1929; Toronto:
        Oxford University Press, 1947; New York: Ungar,
        1957, 1960, pb; New York: Holt Rinehart and
        Winston, 1970.

1315   *Steppenwolf*. Trans. Basil Creighton. Revised by
        Joseph Mileck and Horst Frenz. New York: Holt,
        Rinehart and Winston, 1963, 1966; New York:
        Bantam, 1969, 1972, pb.

HESSE (cont'd).

1316   *Steppenwolf.* Trans. Basil Creighton. Revised
        by Walter Sorell. New York: Modern Library,
        1963; Harmondsworth: Penguin, 1964, pb; London:
        Allen Lane, 1974.

1317   *Strange news from another star, and other tales*
        (Märchen). Trans. Denver Lindley. New York:
        Farrar, Straus and Giroux, 1972, 1974, pb;
        London: Cape, 1973; Harmondsworth: Penguin:1976,
        pb.

1318   *Tales of student life.* Trans. Ralph Manheim.
        New York: Farrar, Straus and Giroux, 1976, pb.

1319   *Wandering: Notes and sketches* (Wanderung: Auf-
        zeichnungen). Trans. James Wright. New York:
        Farrar, Straus and Giroux, 1972, pb; London:
        Cape, 1972; London: Pan Books, 1975, pb.

1320   *Youth, beautiful youth* (Schön ist die Jugend).
        Trans. Richard and Clara Winston. In Pick,
        German stories and tales.

1321   See also: Salinger, *Twentieth century German
        verse*; Kaufmann, *Twenty-five German poets*;
        Francke, *The German classics*, XVIII.

1322   *Autobiographical writings.* Trans. Denver Lindley.
        Ed. Theodore Ziolkowski. New York: Farrar, Straus
        and Giroux, 1972; London: Cape, 1973; London: Pan
        Books, 1975, pb.

1323   *The Hesse/Mann letters: The correspondence of
        Hermann Hesse and Thomas Mann, 1910-1955.* Trans.
        Ralph Manheim. New York: Harper and Row, 1975;
        London: Owen, 1976.

1324   HEYM Georg.

   The autopsy. Trans. Michael Hamburger.   In
   Spender, *Great German short stories.*

1325   Selections in: Hamburger, *Modern German poetry*;
   Hamburger, *German poetry 1910-1975.*

1326   HILDESHEIMER, Wolfgang.

   Nightpiece (Nachtstück).   Trans. Wolfang Hildesheimer.   In Benedikt/Wellwarth, *Postwar German
   theatre.*

1327   *A world ends.*   Trans. Christopher Holme.   In
   Spender, *Great German short stories.*

1328   HOCHHUTH, Rolf.

   The deputy (Der Stellvertreter).   Adapted by
   Jerome Rothenberg.   New York: French, 1964.

1329   *The deputy.*   Trans. Richard and Clara Winston.
   New York: Grove Press, 1964, pb.   Cf. 1330.

1330   *The representative* (Der Stellvertreter).   Trans.
   Robert D. Macdonald.   London: Methuen, 1963;
   Harmondsworth: Penguin, 1969, pb.   Cf. 1228-29.

1331   *Soldiers: An obituary for Geneva* (Soldaten).
   Trans. Robert D. Macdonald.   New York: Grove
   Press; London: Deutsch, 1968; New York: French,
   1969.

1332   HOCHWÄLDER, Fritz.

   The holy experiment (Das heilige Experiment).
   Trans. G.E. Wellwarth.   In Wellwarth, *Themes of
   drama.*

1333   *The public prosecutor* (Der öffentliche Ankläger).
   Trans. Kitty Black.   London, 1958.

HOCHWÄLDER (cont'd).

1334   *The raspberry picker.* Trans. Michael Bullock. In
Corrigan/Esslin, *The new theatre of Europe*, IV.

1335   *The strong are lonely* (Das heilige Experiment).
Adapted by E. La Galliene. New York, 1954;
London, 1956.

1336 HOFMANNSTHAL, Hugo von.
Selected plays and libretti. Ed. Michael Ham-
burger. New York: Pantheon Books, 1963; London:
Routledge and Kegan Paul, 1964. (Electra; The
Salzburg great theatre of the world; The tower;
The cavalier of the rose; Arabella; The difficult
man).

1337   *Selected prose.* Trans. M. Hottinger, Tania and
James Stern. Introd. H. Broch. New York: Pantheon Books; London: Routledge and Kegan Paul, 1952.

1338   *Three plays.* Trans. Alfred Schwarz. Detroit,
Mich.: Wayne State University Press, 1966. (Death
and the fool; Electra; The tower).

1339   *Arabella* (Arabella). Trans. J. Gutmann. New
York: Boosey and Hawkes, 1955.

1340   *Ariadne on Naxos* (Ariadne auf Naxos). Trans. A.
Kalisch. Berlin, 1913; Paris, 1922.

1341   *Death and the fool* (Der Thor und der Tod). Trans.
Michael Hamburger. In Block, *Masters of modern
drama*.

1342   *Death and the fool.* Trans. John Heard. In
Francke, *The German classics*, XVII.

HOFMANNSTHAL (cont'd).

1343   *The death of Titian* (Der Tod des Tizian). Trans.
John Heard. In Francke, *The German classics,* XVII.

1344   *Electra* (Elektra). Trans. A. Kalisch. London:
Boosey and Hawkes, 1953 (1910).

1345   *Electra.* Trans. Carl Richard Mueller. In
Corrigan, *The modern theatre.*

1346   *Electra.* In Corrigan, *Masterpieces of the modern
Central European theatre.*

1347   *An episode in the life of the Marshal de Bassompierre* (Das Erlebnis des Marschalls von Bassompierre). Trans. Mary Hottinger. In Pick, *German
stories and tales.*

1348   *An episode in the life of the Marshal de Bassompierre.* Trans. Mary Hottinger and Tania and
James Stern. In Yuill, *German narrative prose,* II.

1349   *Everyman. Play of the rich man's death* (Jedermann). Trans. G. Sterling and R. Ordynski.
Frankfurt: Fischer, 1954.

1350   *Festival dramas.* Trans. Michael Hamburger. London: Cambridge University Press, 1964.

1351   *The marriage of Sobeide* (Die Hochzeit der Sobeide).
Trans. B.Q. Morgan. In Francke, *The German classics,* XX.

1352   *Poems and verse plays.* Bilingual. Trans. John
Bednall and others. Ed. Michael Hamburger.
Preface T.S. Eliot. London: Routledge and Kegan
Paul; New York: Pantheon Books, 1961.

1353   *The rose bearer* (Der Rosenkavalier). Trans. A.
        Kalisch. Berlin, Paris, 1912; London, 1939.

1354   *The Salzburg everyman* (Jedermann). Salzburg:
        Mora Verlag, 1948.

1355   *A tale of the cavalry* (Reitergeschichte). Trans.
        James Stern. In Spender, *Great German short
        stories*.

1356   Selections in: Flores, *Anthology of German poetry*;
        Salinger, *Twentieth century German verse*; Forster,
        Penguin German verse; Bridgwater, *Twentieth-
        century German verse*; Thomas, *German verse*;
        Kaufmann, *Twenty-five German poets*; Bithell,
        Contemporary German poetry.

1357 HÖLLERER, Walter.
        Selections in: Rothenberg, *New young German poets*.

1358 HOLTHUSEN, Hans Egon.
        The crossing. Trans. Robert Kee and Susi Hughes.
        London: Deutsch, 1959.

1359   See also: Salinger, *Twentieth century German verse*.

1360 HORVÁTH, Ödön von.
        The age of the fish (Zeitalter der Fische). Trans.
        R.W. Thomas. New York: Dial, 1939.

1361   *A child of our time* (Ein Kind unserer Zeit). Trans.
        R.W. Thomas. New York: Dial; London: Methuen, 1939.

1362   *Tales from the Vienna woods* (Geschichten aus dem
        Wienerwald). Trans. Christopher Hampton. London:
        Faber, 1977, pb.

1363 HUBER, Heinz.

The new apartment. Trans. Christopher Holme. In Spender, *Great German short stories*.

1364 HUCH, Ricarda.

The recollections of Ludolf Ursleu the Younger (Erinnerungen von Ludolf Ursleu dem Jüngeren). Trans. Muriel Almon. In Francke, *The German classics*, XVIII.

1365 See also: Salinger, *Twentieth century German verse*.

1366 HUCHEL, Peter.

Selected poems. Bilingual. Trans. Michael Hamburger. Cheadle: Carcanet New Press, 1974, pb.

1367 See also: Hamburger, *German poetry 1910-1975*; Hamburger, *East German poetry*.

1368 JAHNN, Hans Henny.

The ship (Das Holzschiff). Trans. Catherine Hutter. New York: Scribner, 1961; London: Owen, 1970.

1369 JENS, Walter.

The blind man (Der Blinde). Trans. Michael Bullock. New York: Macmillan; London: Deutsch, 1954.

1370 JENTZSCH, Bernd.

Selections in: Hamburger, *East German poetry*; Deicke, *Time for dreams*.

1371 JOHNSON, Uwe.

An absence (Eine Reise wegwohin). Trans. Richard and Clara Winston. London: Cape, 1969; New York: Grossmann, 1970, pb.

JOHNSON (cont'd).

1372 *Anniversaries: From the life of Gesine Cresspahl*
(Jahrestage: Vol. 1 and part of vol 2). Trans.
Leila Vennewitz. New York, London: Harcourt Brace
Jovanovich, 1975. Cf. 1374.

1373 *Berlin, border of the divided world* (Berliner
Stadtbahn). Trans. Ursule Molinaro. In Middleton, *German writing today.*

1374 *Christmas 1967* (Jahrestage: Extract). Trans.
Leila Vennewitz. New York: Harcourt Brace Jovanovich, 1975, 24pp. Cf. 1372.

1375 *Speculations about Jakob* (Mutmassungen über Jakob).
Trans. Ursule Molinaro. New York: Grove Press,
London: Cape, 1963; New York: Harcourt Brace
Jovanovich, 1972, pb.

1376 *The third book about Achim* (Das dritte Buch über
Achim). Trans. Ursule Molinaro. New York: Grove
Press, 1964; New York: Harcourt, Brace and World,
1967; London: Cape, 1968.

1377 *Two views* (Zwei Ansichten). Trans. Richard and
Clara Winston. New York: Harcourt, Brace and
World, 1966; London: Cape, 1967; Harmondsworth:
Penguin, 1971, pb.

1378 JÜNGER, Ernst.
African diversions (Afrikanische Spiele). Trans.
Stuart Hood. London: Lehmann, 1954.

1379 *The glass bees* (Gläserne Bienen). Trans. Louise
Bogan and Elizabeth Mayer. New York: Noonday
Press, 1961, pb.

JÜNGER, Ernst (cont'd).

1380   *On the marble cliffs* (Auf den Marmorklippen).
Trans. Stuart Hood. London: John Lehmann, 1947;
Norfolk, Conn.: New Directions, 1948; Harmonds-
worth: Penguin, 1970, pb.

1381   *Peace* (Der Friede). Trans. Stuart Hood. Chicago:
Regnery, 1948.

1382   *The storm of steel* (In Stahlgewittern). Trans.
B. Creighton. London, Garden City, N.Y., 1929.

1383   JÜNGER, Friedrich Georg.
Selections in: Forster, *Penguin German verse*;
Schwebell, *Contemporary German poetry*.

1384   JUNG, Carl Gustav.
Collected works. Ed. Sir Herbert Read, Michael
Fordham, Gerhard Adler. Trans. R.F.C. Hull.
London: Routledge and Kegan Paul; Princeton, N.J.:
Princeton University Press, 1953-   , 19 vols.

1385   KÄSTNER, Erich.
Let's face it: Poems. Trans. Patrick Bridgwater
and others. London: Cape, 1963.

1386   *A Salzburg comedy* (Der kleine Grenzverkehr).
Trans. C. Brooks. London: Weidenfeld and Nicol-
son; Philadelphia: Saunders, 1950; New York:
Ungar, 1957.

1387   *When I was a little boy* (Als ich ein kleiner
Junge war). Trans. Isabel and Florence McHugh.
London: Cape, 1959; New York: Watts, 1961.

1388   Selections in: Kaufmann, *Twenty-five German poets*.

1389 KAFKA, Franz.

The complete stories. Ed. Nahum N. Glatzer.
New York: Schocken Books, 1971.

1390 *In the penal settlement: Tales and short prose
works* (Gesammelte Schriften. Vol.1: Erzählungen
und kleine Prosa). Trans. Ernst Kaiser and Eithne
Wilkins. London: Secker and Warburg, 1949, 1973.

1391 *The penal colony: Stories and short pieces inclu-
ding The metamorphosis.* Trans. Edwin and Willa
Muir. Epilogue Max Brod. New York: Schocken,
1948, 1959, pb.

1392 *Selected short stories.* Trans. Willa and Edwin
Muir. New York: Modern Library, 1952, pb.

1393 *Shorter works.* Trans. Malcolm Pasley. London:
Secker and Warburg, 1973 (vol.1).

1394 *The trial. America. Tha castle. Metamorphosis. In
the penal settlement. The great wall of China.
Investigations of a dog. Letter to his father.
The diaries.* London: Secker and Warburg/Octopus,
1976.

1395 *Wedding preparations in the country, and other
posthumous prose writings* (Hochzeitsvorbereitungen
auf dem Lande und andere Prose aus dem Nachlass).
Trans. Ernst Kaiser and Eithne Wilkins. London:
Secker and Warburg, 1954, 1973.

1396 *America* (Amerika). Trans. Willa and Edwin Muir.
London: Routledge, 1938; Norfolk, Conn.: New Directions, 1940, 1946, pb; New York: Doubleday, 1955,
pb; Philadelphia; Lippincott; New York: Schocken

KAFKA (cont'd).

Books, 1962, pb; Harmondsworth: Penguin, 1967, pb; London: Secker and Warburg, 1946, 1973.

1397　*The castle* (Das Schloss). Trans. Edwin and Willa Muir. London: Secker and Warburg, 1930, 1953; New York: Knopf, 1930, 1958; (With additional material translated by Eithne Wilkins and Ernst Kaiser.) Harmondsworth: Penguin, 1957, 1974, pb; New York: Knopf, 1956; New York: Watts, 1961; New York: Modern Library, 1969; New York: Schocken, 1974, pb.

1398　*A country doctor* (Ein Landarzt). In Lange, *Great German short novels.*

1399　*Dearest father: Stories and other writings.* Ed. Max Brod. Trans. Ernst Kaiser and Eithne Wilkins. London: Secker and Warburg; New York: Schocken Books; Noonday Press, 1954.

1400　*Description of a struggle* (Beschreibung eines Kampfes). Trans. Tania and James Stern. New York: Schocken Books, 1958.

1401　*Description of a struggle. The great wall of China.* Trans. Willa and Edwin Muir and Tania and James Stern. London: Secker and Warburg, 1960.

1402　*A fasting showman* (Ein Hungerkünstler). Trans. Willa and Edwin Muir. In Yuill, *German narrative prose*, II. Cf. 1405.

1403　*The great wall of China: Stories and reflections* (Beim Bau der chinesischen Mauer). Trans. Willa and Edwin Muir. London: Secker, 1933, 1946; New York: Schocken, 1946, 1970, pb.

KAFKA (cont'd).

1404   *The guardian of the tomb* (Der Gruftwächter).
Trans. J.M. Ritchie. In Ritchie/Garten, *Seven
expressionist plays.*

1405   *A hunger artist* (Ein Hungerkünstler). In Steinhauer, *Twelve German novellas.* Cf. 1402.

1406   *In the penal colony* (In der Strafkolonie). Trans.
Willa and Edwin Muir. In Spender, *Great German
short stories.*

1407   *In the penal settlement.* Trans. Willa and Edwin
Muir. London: Secker and Warburg, 1949.

1408   *The metamorphosis: A critical edition* (Die Ver-
wandlung). Ed. and trans. Stanley Corngold. New
York: Bantam, 1972, pb.

1409   *The metamorphosis.* Trans. Willa and Edwin Muir.
In Pick, *German stories and tales.*

1410   *The metamorphosis.* Bilingual. Trans. Willa and
Edwin Muir. New York: Schocken, 1968 (1948), pb.

1411   *The metamorphosis and other stories.* Trans. Willa
and Edwin Muir. Harmondsworth: Penguin, 1961,
1965, pb.

1412   *Parables* (Parabolen). Bilingual. Trans. Willa
and Edwin Muir and Clement Greenberg. New York:
Schocken, 1947.

1413   *Parables and paradoxes.* Bilingual. Ed. Nahum N.
Glatzer. Trans. Willa and Edwin Muir. New York:
Schocken, 1961, 1970, pb.

KAFKA (cont'd).

1414   *The trial* (Der Prozess). Trans. Willa and Edwin
        Muir. London: Gollancz, 1937; London: Secker and
        Warburg, 1945, 1956; Harmondsworth: Penguin, 1953,
        1974, pb; (rev. and exp. E.M. Butler:) New York:
        Knopf, 1937, 1957; Modern Library, 1964, pb;
        London: Heron Books, 1968; New York: Schocken,
        1968, pb; New York: Vintage, 1969, pb.

1415   *The trial.* Trans. Douglas Scott and Chris
        Waller. Introd. J.P. Stern. London: Pan Books,
        1977, pb.

1416   *Diaries, Vol.1: 1910-1913.* Trans. Joseph Kresh.
        Ed. Max Brod. London: Secker and Warburg; New
        York: Schocken, 1948, pb.

1417   *Diaries, Vol.II: 1914-1923.* Ed. Max Brod. Trans.
        Martin Greenberg, with Hannah Arendt. London:
        Secker and Warburg; New York: Schocken, 1949, pb.

1418   *The diaries of Franz Kafka: 1910-1923* (selections).
        Trans. Joseph Kresh, Martin Greenberg and Hannah
        Arendt. Harmondsworth: Penguin, 1964, 1972, pb.

1419   *I am a memory come alive* (autobiographical writings).
        Ed. Nahum N. Glatzer. New York: Schocken, 1974.

1420   *Letters to Felice* (Briefe an Felice). Ed. Erich
        Heller and Jürgen Born. Trans. James Stern and
        Elizabeth Duckworth. New York: Schocken Books,
        1973; London: Secker and Warburg, 1974.

1421   *Letters to friends, family, and editors.* Trans.
        Richard and Clara Winston. New York: Schocken,
        1977; London: Calder, 1978.

KAFKA (cont'd).

1422   *Letters to Milena* (Briefe an Milena). Trans. Tania and James Stern. London: Secker and Warburg, 1953; New York: Schocken, 1954, pb; London: Transworld/Corgi, 1967, pb.

1423   *Letter to his father* (Brief an den Vater). Bilingual. Trans. Ernst Kaiser and Eithne Wilkins. New York: Schocken, 1966, 1970, pb.

1424   See also: Lamport, *German short stories*.

1425 KAHLAU, Heinz.
Selections in: Hamburger, *East German poetry*; Deicke, *Time for dreams*.

1426 KAISER, Georg.
Five plays. Trans. B.J. Kenworthy, Rex Last and J.M. Ritchie. London: Calder and Boyars, 1971.

1427   *Alkibiades saved* (Der gerettete Alkibiades). Trans. B.Q. Morgan. In Sokel, *Anthology of German expressionist drama*.

1428   *The coral: A play* (Die Koralle). Trans. Winifred Katzin. Introd. Victor Lange. New York: Ungar, 1963, pb.

1429   *From morn to midnight* (Von morgens bis mitternachts). Trans. Ashley Dukes. London, 1920; New York, 1922.

1430   *From morn to midnight*. Trans. Ashley Dukes. In Block, *Masters of modern drama*.

1431   *From morn to midnight*. Trans. Ashley Dukes. In Gassner, *Twenty best European plays*.

KAISER (cont'd).

1432   *From morn to midnight*. Trans. Ashley Dukes.   In
Moses, *Dramas of modernism*.

1433   *From morn to midnight*. Trans. Ulrich Weisstein.
In Brockett, *Plays for the theatre*.

1434   *Gas I: A play* (Gas I). Trans. Herman Scheffauer.
Introd. Victor Lange. Boston, 1924; New York:
Ungar, 1957, 1963, pb.

1435   *Gas II: A play* (Gas II). Trans. Winifred Katzin.
Introd. Victor Lange. New York: Ungar, 1963, pb.

1436   *The protagonist* (Der Protagonist). Trans. H.F.
Garten.   In Ritchie/Garten, *Seven expressionist
plays*.

1437   *The raft of the Medusa* (Das Floss der Medusa).
Trans. George E. Wellwarth.   In Benedikt/Wellwarth,
Postwar German theatre.

1438 KASACK, Hermann.
The city beyond the river (Die Stadt hinter dem
Strom). Trans. Peter de Mendelssohn.   London:
Longmans, Green, 1953.

1439 KELLERMANN, Bernhard.
God's beloved. Trans. Katharine Royce.   In Francke,
The German classics, XX.

1440 KESTEN, Hermann.
Casanova (Casanova). Trans. James Stern and
Robert Pick. New York: Harper, 1955; Collier,
1962, pb; London: New English Library, 1963, pb.

1441   *Happy man* (Glückliche Menschen). Trans. Edward
Crankshaw. New York: Wyn, 1947

KESTEN (cont'd).

1442　*The twins of Nuremberg* (Die Zwillinge von Nürnberg).
Trans. Andrew St. James and E.B. Ashton. New York:
Fischer, 1946.

1443　KEYSERLING, Eduard von.
Gay hearts (Bunte Herzen). Trans. B.Q. Morgan.
In Francke, *The German classics*, XIX.

1444　KIPPHARDT, Heinar.
In the matter of J. Robert Oppenheimer (In der
Sache J. Robert Oppenheimer). Trans. Ruth Speirs.
London: Methuen, 1967, pb.

1445　KIRSCH, Sarah.
Selections in: Hamburger, *East German poetry*;
Deicke, *Time for dreams*.

1446　KIRST, Hans Hellmut.
Brothers in arms (Kameraden). Trans. J.M. Brownjohn. New York: Harper, 1967.

1447　*Forward, gunner Asch.* Trans. Robert Kee. New
York: Pyramid Books, 1956, pb.

1448　*The night of the generals* (Die Nacht der Generale).
Trans. J.M. Brownjohn. New York: Harper, 1964;
Bantam, 1964, pb.

1449　*The officer factory* (Fabrik der Offiziere).
Trans. Robert Kee. New York: Pyramid Books, 1963,
pb.

1450　*The return of gunner Asch.* Trans. Robert Kee.
New York: Pyramid Books, 1957, pb.

1451　*The revolt of gunner Asch* (Null-acht-fünfzehn in

KIRST (cont'd).

der Kaserne). Trans. Robert Kee. New York:
Little; Pyramid Books, 1956, pb.

1452 *Soldier's revolt.* Trans. J.M. Brownjohn. New
York: Harper, 1966; Bantam, 1966, pb.

1453 *What became of gunner Asch.* Trans. J.M. Brownjohn.
New York: Harper, 1965; Pyramid Books, 1965, pb.

1454 KISCH, Egon Erwin.
Tales from seven ghettos (Geschichten aus sieben
Ghettos). Trans. E. Bone. London: Anscombe, 1948.

1455 KLABUND.
The circle of chalk (Der Kreidekreis). Trans. J.
Laver. London: Heinemann, 1929.

1456 Selections in: Kaufmann, *Twenty-five German poets.*

1457 KLEE, Paul.
Selections in: Watts, *Three painter-poets.*

1458 KLUGE, Alexander.
Attendance list for a funeral: Stories (Lebens-
läufe). Trans. Leila Vennewitz. New York:
McGraw-Hill, 1966.

1459 *The battle* (Schlachtbeschreibung). Trans. Leila
Vennewitz. New York: McGraw-Hill, 1967.

1460 KOEPPEN, Wolfgang.
Death in Rome (Tod in Rom). Trans. Mervyn Savill,
London: Weidenfeld and Nicolson, 1956; New York:
Vanguard Press, 1961, pb.

1461 KOKOSCHKA, Oskar.
Job (Hiob). Trans. Michael Benedikt. In Wellwarth,
German drama between the wars.

KOKOSCHKA (cont'd).

1462   *Job.* Trans. Walter H. and Jacqueline Sokel. In
        Sokel, *Anthology of German expressionist drama.*

1463   *Murderer hope of womankind* (Mörder Hoffnung der
        Frauen). Trans. J.M. Ritchie. In Ritchie/Garten,
        Seven expressionist plays.

1464   *Murderer the women's hope* (Mörder Hoffnung der
        Frauen). Trans. Michael Hamburger. In Sokel,
        Anthology of German expressionist drama.

1465   *A sea ringed with visions* (Spur im Treibsand).
        Trans. Eithne Wilkins and Ernst Kaiser. London:
        Thames and Hudson; New York: Horizon Press, 1962.

1466   KOLBENHEYER, E.G.
        A winter chronicle (Meister Joachim Pausewang).
        Trans. H.A. Phillips and K.-W. Maurer. London:
        Bodley Head, 1938.

1467   KOLMAR, Gertrud.
        Dark Soliloquy: Selected poems. Bilingual. Trans.
        Henry A. Smith. New York: Seabury Press, 1975.

1468   *Selected poems.* Trans. David Kipp. London:
        Magpie Press, 1970, pb.

1469   KRAUS, Karl.
        No compromise: Selected writings. Ed. Frederick
        Ungar. Trans. Sheema Z. Buehne and others. New
        York: Ungar, 1977.

1470   *The last days of mankind* (Die letzten Tage der
        Menschheit). Trans. Alexander Gode and Sue Ellen
        Wright. Ed. Frederick Ungar. New York: Ungar,
        1974.

KRAUS (cont'd).

1471   *The last days of mankind* (extract). Trans. Max
        Spalter. In Wellwarth, *German drama between the*
        wars.

1472   KROETZ, Franz Xaver.
        Farmyard, and four other plays. Introd. Richard
        Gilman. Trans. Michael Roloff and others. New
        York: Urizen Books, 1976.

1473   *Stallerhof* (Stallerhof). Trans. Katharina Helm.
        In: Wolfgang Bauer, *Shakespeare the sadist*
        (London: Eyre Methuen, 1977, pb).

1474   KROLOW, Karl.
        Foreign bodies: Poems (Fremde Körper). Bilingual.
        Trans. Michael Bullock. Athens: Ohio Unversity
        Press, 1969.

1475   *Invisible hands* (Unsichtbare Hände). Trans.
        Michael Bullock. London: Cape Goliard Press,
        1969; New York: Grossman, 1969, pb.

1476   *Poems against death.* Trans. Herman Salinger.
        Washington: Charioteer, 1969.

1477   See also: Rothenberg, *New young German poets*;
        Hamburger, *German poetry 1910-1975*; Schwebell,
        Contemporary German poetry.

1478   KUBIN, Alfred.
        The other side: A fantastic novel (Die andere
        Seite). Trans. Denver Lindley. New York: Crown
        Publishers, 1967; London: Gollancz, 1969; Har-
        mondsworth: Penguin, 1973, pb.

1479 KUBY, Erich.
The sitzkrieg of private Stefan (Sieg! Sieg!).
Trans. Theodore H. Lustig. New York: Farrar,
Straus, 1962.

1480 KUNERT, Günter.
Selections in: Hamburger, *East German poetry*;
Deicke, *Time for dreams*.

1481 KUNZE, Reiner.
With the volume turned down, and other poems
(Zimmerlautstärke). Trans. Ewald Osers. London:
London Magazine Editions, 1973, pb.

1482 *The wonderful years* (Die wunderbaren Jahre).
Trans. Joachim Neugroschel. New York: Braziller,
1977.

1483 Selections in: Hamburger, *East German poetry*;
Deicke, *Time for dreams*.

1484 KURZ, Isolde.
Selections in: Salinger, *Twentieth century
German verse*.

1485 LANGGÄSSER, Elisabeth.
The quest (Märkische Argonautenfahrt). Trans.
J.B. Greene. New York: Knopf, 1953.

1486 LASKER-SCHÜLER, Else.
Selections in: Deutsch, *Contemporary German poetry*;
Bithell, *Contemporary German poetry*.

1487 LASZLO, Carl.
The Chinese icebox (Der chinesische Kühlschrank).
Trans. George E. Wellwarth. In Benedikt/Wellwarth,
Postwar German theatre.

LASZLO (cont'd).

1488   *Let's eat hair!* (Essen wir Haare). Trans. George
E. Wellwarth. In Benedikt/Wellwarth, *Postwar
German theatre.*

1489   LAUCKNER, Rolf.
Cry in the street (Schrei aus der Strasse). Trans.
Maurice Edwards and Valerie Reich. In Sokel,
Anthology of German expressionist drama.

1490   LAVANT, Christine.
Selections in: Schwebell, *Contemporary German
poetry.*

1491   LeFORT, Gertrud von.
Eternal Woman (Die ewige Frau). Trans. M.C.
Buehrle. Milwaukee: Bruce, 1954.

1492   *The judgement of the sea* (Das Gericht des Meeres).
Trans. Isabel and Florence McHugh. In Yuill,
German narrative prose, II.

1493   *The judgement of the sea: Four novellas.* Trans.
Isabel and Florence McHugh. Chicago: Regnery, 1962.

1494   *The song at the scaffold* (Die Letzte am Schafott).
Trans. Olga Marx. New York: Sheed and Ward, 1951;
London: Sheed and Ward, 1953; New York: Doubleday,
1961, pb.

1495   *The veil of Veronica* (Das Schweisstuch der Veronika).
Trans. Conrad M.R. Bonacina. New York: AMS Press,
1970.

1496   *The wife of Pilate* (Die Frau des Pilatus). Trans.
Marie C. Buehrle. Milwaukee, Wis,: Bruce, 1957, pb.

1497 LENZ, Siegfried.

      An exemplary life (Das Vorbild). Trans. Douglas Parmée. New York: Hill and Wang; London: Secker and Warburg, 1976.

1498 *The German lesson* (Deutschstunde). Trans. Ernst Kaiser and Eithne Wilkins. London: Macdonald, 1971; New York: Hill and Wang, 1972.

1499 *The lightship* (Das Feuerschiff). Trans. Michael Bullock. New York: Hill and Wang, 1962; London: Heinemann, 1964; New York: Bantam, 1967.

1500 *Luke, gentle servant* (Lukas, sanftmütiger Knecht). Trans. Kathrine Talbot. In Middleton, *German writing today*.

1501 *The survivor*. Trans. Michael Bullock. New York: Hill and Wang, 1965.

1502 LERNET-Holenia, Alexander.

      Count Luna. Two tales of the real and the unreal (Der Graf Luna. Der Baron Bagge). Trans. R. and C. Winston and J.B. Greene. New York: Criterion Books, 1956; London: Blond, 1960.

1503 See also: Pick, *German stories and tales*.

1504 LERSCH, Heinrich.

      Selections in: Salinger, *Twentieth century German verse*.

1505 LETTAU, Reinhard.

      Enemies (Feinde). Trans. Agnes Rook. London: Calder and Boyars, 1973.

1506 *Obstacles*. Trans. Ursule Molinaro and Ellen Sutton. New York: Pantheon Books, 1965; London: Calder and Boyars, 1966.

LETTAU (cont'd),

1507   See also: Newnham, *German short stories.*

1508   LICHTENSTEIN, Alfred.
        Selections in: Hamburger, *Modern German poetry*;
        Hamburger, *German poetry 1910-1975.*

1509   LIND, Jakov.
        Ergo (Eine bessere Welt). Trans. Ralph Manheim.
        London: Methuen; New York: Random, 1967; New
        York: Hill and Wang, 1968, pb.

1510   *Landscape in concrete* (Landschaft in Beton).
        Trans. Ralph Manheim. London: Methuen, 1966;
        New York: Grove Press, 1966; New York: Pocket
        Books, Inc., 1968, pb.

1511   *The silver foxes are dead, and other plays: Anna
        Laub, Hunger, Fear.* Trans. Ralph Manheim. London:
        Methuen, 1968; New York: Hill and Wang, 1969, pb.

1512   *Soul of wood, and other stories* (Eine Seele aus
        Holz). Trans. Ralph Manheim. London: Cape, 1964;
        New York: Grove Press, 1965; Greenwich, Conn.:
        Fawcett, 1966; London: Panther, 1967, pb.

1513   MANN, Heinrich.
        Abdication. Trans. Lawrence Wilson. In Yuill,
        German narrative prose, II.

1514   *The blue angel* (Professor Unrat). A modern ren-
        dition and adaptation by Wirt Williams. London:
        Jarrolds, 1932; New York: New American Library,
        1959, pb; London: Hamilton, 1959; New York: Fertig,
        1976.

MANN, Heinrich (cont'd).

1515 *Little superman*. Trans. Ernest Boyd. New York: Creative Age, 1945.

1516 *The little town* (Die kleine Stadt). Trans. Winifred Ray. London: Secker, 1930; New York: Ungar, 1962, pb.

1517 *Man of straw* (Der Untertan). London: Hutchinson, 1947; London: Sphere Books, 1972, pb. Cf. 1518.

1518 *The patrioteer* (Der Untertan). Trans. E. Boyd. New York, 1921. Cf. 1517.

1519 *Three minute novel*. In Lange, *Great German short novels*.

1520 MANN, Klaus.
Mephisto (Mephisto). Trans. Robin Smyth. New York: Random House, 1977.

1521 *Pathetic symphony* (Symphonie pathétique). New York: Crown Publishers, 1948.

1522 MANN, Thomas.
Children and fools (selected short fiction). Trans. Herman George Scheffauer. New York: Knopf, 1928; Freeport, N.Y.: Books for Libraries Press, 1970.

1523 *Death in Venice and seven other stories*. Trans. H.T. Lowe-Porter. New York: Random House (Vintage Books), 1954, 1963, pb.

1524 *Death in Venice. Tristan. Tonio Kröger*. Trans. H.T. Lowe-Porter. Harmondsworth: Penguin, 1955 (1928), 1964, pb.

MANN, Thomas (cont'd).

1525   *Essays of three decades.* Trans. H.T. Lowe-Porter.
        New York: Knopf, 1947; New York: Vintage, 1957,
        1958.

1526   *Last essays.* Trans. Richard and Clara Winston,
        and Tania and James Stern, also H.T. Lowe-Porter.
        London: Secker; New York: Knopf, 1959.

1527   *Selections.* Ed. F. Walter. London, New York:
        Macmillan, 1948-49, pb.

1528   *Stories and episodes.* Introd. Erich Heller.
        London: Dent; New York: Dutton, 1940, 1955.

1529   *Stories of a lifetime. The collected stories.*
        2 vols. London: Secker and Warburg; Mercury
        Books, 1961.

1530   *Stories of three decades.* Trans. H.T. Lowe-Porter.
        New York: Knopf, 1936; Random House, 1961, pb.

1531   *The Thomas Mann reader.* Ed. Joseph Warner Angell.
        Trans. H.T. Lowe-Porter and others. New York:
        Knopf, 1950; New York: Grosset and Dunlap, 1957, pb.

1532   *The beloved returns* (Lotte in Weimar). Trans. H.T.
        Lowe-Porter. New York: Knopf, 1940, 1957. Cf. 1551.

1533   *The black swan* (Die Betrogene). Trans. W.R. Trask.
        New York: Knopf; London: Secker and Warburg, 1954.

1534   *Buddenbrooks* (Buddenbrooks). Trans. H.T. Lowe-
        Porter. New York: Knopf, 1924; London: Secker,
        1924, 1956; New York: Pocket Books, 1952, pb. Har-
        mondsworth: Penguin, 1957, 1975, pb; New York:
        Vintage Books, 1961, pb; New York: Knopf, 1964.

MANN, Thomas (cont'd).

1535   *The buffoon* (Der Bajazzo). In Steinhauer, *Twelve German novellas.*

1536   *Confessions of Felix Krull, confidence man* (Bekenntnisse des Hochstaplers Felix Krull). Trans. Denver Lindley. New York: Knopf, 1955; Harmondsworth: Penguin, 1958, pb; New York: New American Library, 1963, pb; New York: Modern Library, 1965; London: Secker and Warburg, 1955, 1977.

1537   *Death in Venice* (Der Tod in Venedig). Trans. Kenneth Burke. New York: Knopf, 1925, 1965; New York: Modern Library, 1954, 1970, pb; New York: Stinehour Press, 1972.

1538   *Death in Venice.* Trans. Kenneth Burke. In Cerf, *German short novels and stories.*

1539   *Death in Venice.* In Lange, *Great German short novels.*

1540   *Death in Venice.* Trans. H.T. Lowe-Porter. London: Secker, 1928; Harmondsworth: Penguin, 1971, pb.

1541   *Death in Venice.* Trans. H.T. Lowe-Porter. In Pick, *German stories and tales.*

1542   *Doctor Faustus* (Doktor Faustus). Trans. H.T. Lowe-Porter. New York: Knopf, 1948, 1952; London: Secker and Warburg, 1949; New York: Modern Library, 1966; Harmondsworth: Penguin, 1968, pb; New York: Random House (Vintage), 1971, pb.

1543   *Germany and the Germans.* Washington: Library of Congress, 1945.

MANN, Thomas, (cont'd).

1544   *Gladius Dei* (Gladius Dei). Trans. H.T. Lowe-
Porter. In Spender, *Great German short stories.*

1545   *Goethe and democracy* (Goethe und die Demokratie).
Washington: Library of Congress, 1950.

1546   *The holy sinner* (Der Erwählte). Trans. H.T. Lowe-
Porter. New York: Knopf, 1951; London: Secker and
Warburg, 1952; Harmondsworth: Penguin, 1961, 1972,
pb.

1547   *Joseph and his brothers* (Joseph und seine Brüder).
Trans. H.T. Lowe-Porter. New York, 1934-44, 4 vols.
See: *The tales of Jacob; Young Joseph; Joseph in
Egypt; Joseph the provider.*

1548   *Joseph in Egypt* (Joseph in Ägypten). Trans. H.T.
Lowe-Porter. London: Secker and Warburg, 1938;
London: Sphere, 1968, pb. VoL 3 of *Joseph and
his brothers.* Cf. 1547.

1549   *Joseph the provider* (Joseph der Ernährer). Trans.
H.T. Lowe-Porter. London: Secker and Warburg,
1945; London: Sphere, 1968, pb. VoL 4 of *Joseph
and his brothers.* Cf. 1547.

1550   *Little Herr Friedemann, and other stories* (Der
kleine Herr Friedemann). Harmondsworth: Penguin,
1972, pb.

1551   *Lotte in Weimar* (Lotte in Weimar). Trans. H.T.
Lowe-Porter. London: Secker and Warburg, 1940;
Harmondsworth: Penguin, 1968, 1976, pb. Cf. 1532.

1552   *The magic mountain* (Der Zauberberg). Trans. H.T.
Lowe-Porter. New York: Knopf; London: Secker and

MANN, Thomas (cont'd).

Warburg, 1927; Harmondsworth, Baltimore: Penguin,
1960, pb; New York: Heritage Press, 1962; New York:
Vintage Books, 1967, 1969, pb.

1553 *Mario and the magician, and other stories* (Mario
und der Zauberer). Trans. H.T. Lowe-Porter.
Harmondsworth: Penguin, 1975, pb.

1554 *Nocturnes* (A gleam; Railway accident; A weary
hour). New York: Equinox, 1934; New York: Books
for Libraries Press, 1970.

1555 *Past masters, and other papers.* Trans. H.T. Lowe-
Porter. New York: Knopf, 1933; Freeport, N.Y.:
Books for Libraries Press, 1968.

1556 *Royal Highness* (Königliche Hoheit). Trans. A.
Cecil Curtis. Revised by Constance McNab. New
York: 1916, 1939; London: New English Library,
1962, pb; Harmondsworth: Penguin, 1975, 1979, pb.

1557 *A sketch of my life* (Lebensabriss). Trans. H.T.
Lowe-Porter. Paris: Harrison, 1930; New York:
Knopf, 1960.

1558 *The tables of the law* (Das Gesetz). Trans. H.T.
Lowe-Porter. New York: Knopf, 1945.

1559 *The tales of Jacob* (Die Geschichten Jaakobs). Trans.
H.T. Lowe-Porter. London: Secker and Warburg, 1934;
London: Sphere, 1968, pb. Vol. 1 of *Joseph and
his brothers.* Cf. 1547.

1560 *Tonio Kröger and other stories.* Trans. David
Luke. New York: Bantam, 1970, pb.

MANN, Thomas (cont'd).

1561   *Tonio Kröger* (Tonio Kröger). Trans. B.Q. Morgan.
In Francke, *The German classics*, XIX.

1562   *The transposed heads* (Die vertauschten Köpfe).
Trans. H.T. Lowe-Porter. New York: Knopf, 1941;
Vintage Books, 1959, pb.

1563   *The transposed heads. The black swan.* Trans. H.T.
Lowe-Porter and W.R. Trask. Calcutta: Rupa, 1961.

1564   *Young Joseph* (Der junge Joseph). Trans. H.T.
Lowe-Porter. London: Secker and Warburg, 1935;
London: Sphere, 1968, pb. Vol. 2 of *Joseph and
his brothers.* Cf. 1547.

1565   *Letters of Thomas Mann, 1889-1955.* Sel. and trans.
Richard and Clara Winston. London: Secker and
Warburg, 1970; New York: Knopf, 1970; Harmonds-
worth: Penguin, 1975, pb.

1566   *Letters to Paul Amann.* Trans. R. and C. Winston.
Ed. H. Wegener. Middleton, Conn.: Wesleyan University Press, 1960.

1567   See also: *The Hesse/Mann letters* (1285); Lamport,
German short stories.

1568 MECKEL, Christoph.
Selections in: Hamburger, *German poetry 1910-1975.*

1569 MEISTER, Ernst.
Selections in: Hamburger, *German poetry 1910-1975.*

1570 MELL, Max.
Apostle play (Das Apostelspiel). Trans. M.U.
White. London, 1934.

1571 MICHEL, Karl.
Selections in: Hamburger, *East German poetry*;
Deicke, *Time for dreams*.

1572 MIEGEL, Agnes.
Selections in: Salinger, *Twentieth century German
verse*; Bithell, *Contemporary German poetry*.

1573 MOMBERT, Alfred.
Selections in: Deutsch. *Contemporary German poetry*;
Bithell, *Contemporary German poetry*.

1574 MORGENSTERN, Christian.
Selected poems of Christian Morgenstern. Trans.
Alfred Feiner. Walton-on-Thames: Outposts Pub-
lishers, 1973, pb.

1575 *The daynight lamp*. Bilingual. Trans. Max Knight.
Boston: Houghton Mifflin, 1973.

1576 *The gallows songs* (Galgenlieder). Bilingual.
Trans. Max Knight. London: Cambridge University
Press; Berkeley, Ca.: University of California
Press, 1964, pb.

1577 *Gallows songs*. Trans. W.D. Snodgrass and Lore
Segal. Ann Arbor: University of Michigan Press,
1967.

1578 *The great Lalula, and other nonsense rhymes* (Galgenlieder: Extracts). Trans. Max Knight. New
York: Putnam, 1969.

1579 *The moon sheep* (Das Mondschaf). Bilingual. Trans.
A.E.W. Eitzen. Wiesbaden: Insel Verlag, 1953.

1580 *The three sparrows*. Trans. Max Knight. New York:
Scribner, 1968.

MORGENSTERN (cont'd).

1581   Selections in: Flores, *Anthology of German poetry*;
Salinger, *Twentieth century German verse*; Forster,
Penguin German verse; Kaufmann, *Twenty-five German
poets*; Deutsch, *Contemporary German poetry*.

1582 MUSIL, Robert.

Five women. Unions (Drei Frauen. Vereinigungen).
Trans. Eithne Wilkins and Ernst Kaiser. New York:
Delacorte Press, 1966.

1583   *The man without qualities* (Der Mann ohne Eigen-
schaften). Trans. Eithne Wilkins and Ernst
Kaiser. New York: Putnam, 1965, 3 vols., pb.

1584   *The man without qualities. Vols. 1-2.* Trans.
Eithne Wilkins and Ernst Kaiser. London: Secker
and Warburg; New York: Coward McCann, 1953-54,
1979; London: Panther Books, 1968, pb; London:
Pan Books/Picador, 1979, pb.

1585   *The man without qualities. Vol. 3: Into the
millenium (The criminals).* Trans. Eithne Wilkins
and Ernst Kaiser. London: Secker and Warburg,
1960, 1979; London: Panther Books, 1968, pb;
London: Pan Books/Picador, 1979, pb.

1586   *Tonka, and other stories.* Trans. Eithne Wilkins
and Ernst Kaiser. London: Secker and Warburg,
1965; Panther Books, 1969, pb.

1587   *Young Törless* (Die Verwirrungen des Zöglings Törless). Trans. Eithne Wilkins and Ernst Kaiser. New
York: Pantheon Books; London: Secker and Warburg,
1955; New York: Noonday Press, 1958, pb; Harmondsworth: Penguin, 1961, pb; New York: New American
Library, 1964, pb; London: Panther Books, 1971, 1979,pb.

1588 NEUMANN, Alfred.
      Such men are dangerous (Der Patriot). Adapted by
      Ashley Dukes. New York and London, 1928.

1589 NOSSACK, Hans Erich.
      The D'Arthez case (Der Fall d'Arthez). Trans.
      Michael Lebeck. New York: Farrar, Straus and
      Giroux, 1971.

1590 *The impossible proof* (Unmögliche Beweisafunahme).
      Trans. Michael Lebeck. New York: Farrar, Straus
      and Giroux, 1968; London: Barrie and Rockcliff,
      1969.

1591 *The marker* (Das Mal). Trans. Kathrine Talbot.
      In Middleton, *German writing today*.

1592 *The meeting in the hallway* (Begegnung im Vorraum).
      Trans. Christopher Middleton. In Spender, *Great
      German short stories*.

1593 *To the unknown hero* (Dem unbekannten Sieger).
      Trans. Ralph Manheim. New York: Farrar, Straus
      and Giroux, 1974; London: Alcove Press, 1974.

1594 PENZOLDT, Ernst.
      The treasure. Trans. A.J. Pomerans. In Yuill,
      German narrative prose, II.

1595 PIONTEK, Heinz.
      Selections in: Hamburger, *Modern German poetry*;
      Hamburger, *German poetry 1910-1975*; Rothenberg,
      New young German poets.

1596 PLIEVIER, Theodor.
      Berlin (Berlin). Trans. Louis Hagen and Vivian
      Milroy. London: Hammond, 1956; New York: Doubleday,

PLIEVIER (cont'd).

1957; New York: Ace Books, 1959, pb; Chester
Springs: Dufour, 1966; St. Albans: Mayflower, 1976,
pb.

1597   *Moscow* (Moskau). Trans. Stuart Hood. London:
Mueller, 1953; New York: Doubleday, 1954; London:
Hamilton, 1956; New York: Ace Books, 1962, pb;
New York: Berkeley, 1958; St. Albans: Mayflower,
1967, pb.

1598   *Stalingrad* (Stalingrad). Trans. H.L. Robinson.
London: Athenaeum Press; New York: Appleton-
Century-Crofts, 1948; London: Hamilton, 1956,
1959, pb.

1599   *Stalingrad.* Trans. Richard and Clara Winston.
New York: Royal Books, 1952; New York: Berkeley
Publications, 1964, pb; New York: Time, 1966.

1600   *The world's last corner* (Im letzten Winkel der
Erde). Trans. Robert Pick. New York: Appleton-
Century-Crofts, 1951.

1601   PREISSLER, Helmut.
Selections in: Deicke, *Time for dreams.*

1602   REMARQUE, Erich Maria.
All quiet on the Western Front (Im Westen nichts
Neues). Trans. A.W. Wheen. London: Putnam,
1929, 1948; Greenwich, Conn.: Fawcett World,
1958, 1968, pb; Boston: Little, 1958; London:
Folio Society, 1966; New York: Limited Editions
Club, 1969; London: Heinemann, 1970.

REMARQUE (cont'd).

1603   *Arch of triumph* (Arc de triomphe). Trans. Walter
Sorrell and Denver Lindley. New York: Appleton-
Century-Crofts, 1945; Grosset and Dunlap, 1947;
New York: New American Library; London: Hutchinson,
1950; London: Hamilton, 1961, pb; Greenwich, Conn.:
Fawcett Publ., 1962, pb; New York: Avon Books,
1971; London: Hutchinson, 1972.

1604   *The black obelisk* (Der schwarze Obelisk). Trans.
Denver Lindley. New York: Harcourt, Brace, 1957;
London: Hutchinson, 1957; London: Four Square
Books, 1961, pb; Greenwich, Conn.: Fawcett Publ.,
1964, pb.

1605   *Flotsam* (Liebe deinen Nächsten). Trans. Denver
Lindley. London: Hutchinson, 1941; London: H.
Hamilton, 1961, 1964, pb.

1606   *Heaven has no favourites* (Der Himmel kennt keine
Günstlinge). Trans. Richard and Clara Winston.
London: Hutchinson, 1961; New York: Harcourt,
Brace, 1961; Greenwich, Conn.: Fawcett Publ.,
1964, pb.

1607   *The night in Lisbon* (Die Nacht von Lissabon).
Trans. Ralph Manheim. New York: Harcourt, Brace;
London: Hutchinson, 1964; Greenwich, Conn.: Fawcett,
1965; London: Hutchinson, 1972.

1608   *The road back* (Der Weg zurück). Trans. A.W.
Wheen. New York: Avon Press, 1964, pb.

1609   *Shadows in Paradise* (Schatten im Paradies). Trans.
Ralph Manheim. New York: Harcourt Brace Jovanovich; London: Hutchinson, 1972.

REMARQUE (cont'd).

1610 *Spark of life* (Der Funke Leben). Trans. J. Stern.
New York: Appleton-Century-Crofts; London: Hutchinson, 1952; New York: New American Library,
1953, pb; New York: Dell Publ., 1964, pb.

1611 *Three comrades* (Drei Kameraden). Trans. A.W.
Wheen. London: Hutchinson, 1937; Boston: Little,
Brown, 1946; London: World Distrib., 1961, pb;
New York: Popular Library, 1953, 1964, pb; Lon-
don: Sphere Books, 1967.

1612 *A time to love and a time to die* (Zeit zu lieben
und Zeit zu sterben). Trans. Denver Lindley.
New York: Harcourt, Brace, 1954; London: Hutchinson, 1954; New York: Popular Library, 1955, 1966,
pb; London: H. Hamilton, 1961, pb.

1613 RICHTER, Hans Werner.
Beyond defeat (Die Geschlagenen). Trans. R. Kee.
New York: Putnam; Aldershot, Hants.: MacGibbon
and Kee, 1950; London: H. Hamilton, 1960, pb
(British edn.: *Odds against us*).

1614 *They fell from God's hand* (Sie fielen aus Gottes
Hand). Trans. Geoffrey Sainsbury. London:
Harrap; New York: Dutton, 1956; London: World
Distr., 1957, pb; Morley, Elmfield Press, 1973.

1615 RILKE, Rainer Maria.
Five prose pieces. Trans. Carl Niemeyer. Cummington, Mass.: Cummington, 1947.

1616 *New poems.* Bilingual. Trans. J.B. Leishman.
London: Hogarth, 1964; New York: New Directions,
1964.

RILKE (cont'd).

1617　　*Poems 1906 to 1926*. Trans. James B. Leishman.
　　　　London: Hogarth Press, 1934, 1957; Norfolk, Conn.:
　　　　New Directions, 1957.

1618　　*Possibility of being: A selection of poems*. Trans.
　　　　J.B. Leishman. New York: New Directions, 1977.

1619　　*Rilke on love and other difficulties*. Trans.
　　　　John J.L. Mood. New York: Norton, 1975.

1620　　*Selected letters*. Ed. Harry T. Moore. Trans.
　　　　J.B. Greene and N. Herter. New York: Doubleday,
　　　　1960, pb.

1621　　*Selected poems*. Trans. James B. Leishman. Lon-
　　　　don: Hogarth Press, 1941; Harmondworth: Penguin,
　　　　1964, pb.

1622　　*Selected poems*. Bilingual. Trans. C.F. MacIntyre.
　　　　London: Cambridge University Press; Berkeley, Ca.:
　　　　Univeristy of California Press, 1947, 1960, pb.

1623　　*Selected works*. *Vol.1: Prose*. Trans. G.C.
　　　　Houston. London: Hogarth Press, 1954; Norfolk,
　　　　Conn.: New Directions, 1960.

1624　　*Selected works*. *Vol.2: Poetry*. Trans. James B.
　　　　Leishman. London: Hogarth Press, 1960; Norfolk,
　　　　Conn.: New Directions, 1960.

1625　　*Thirty-one poems by Rainer Maria Rilke*. Trans.
　　　　Ludwig Lewisohn. New York: Ackerman, 1946.

1626　　*Translations from the poetry of Rainer Maria
　　　　Rilke*. Bilingual. Trans. M.D. Herter Norton.
　　　　New York: Norton, 1962, pb.

RILKE (cont'd).

1627 *Angel songs* (Engellieder). Trans. Rhoda Coghill.
Dublin: Dolmen Press, 1958.

1628 *The book of hours* (Stundenbuch). Trans. A.L. Peck.
London: Hogarth Press, 1961; Chester Springs, Pa.:
Dufour Editions, 1964. Cf. 1648.

1629 *The cornet* (Weise von Liebe und Tod des Cornets
Christoph Rilke). Trans. Constantine Fitzgibbon.
London: Wingate, 1958.

1630 *Duinesian elegies* (Duineser Elegien). Bilingual.
Trans. Elaine E. Boney. Chapel Hill: University
of North Carolina Press, 1975.

1631 *The Duino elegies* (Duineser Elegien). Trans.
Harry Behn. Mt. Vernon, N.Y.: Peter Pauper Press,
1957.

1632 *Duino elegies*. Bilingual. Trans., introd., and
comm. James B. Leishman and Stephen Spender.
London: Hogarth Press, 1939, 1957; New York:
Norton, 1939, 1963, pb.

1633 *Duino elegies*. Bilingual. Trans. C.F. MacIntyre.
Berkeley, Ca.: University of California Press,
1961, pb.

1634 *The Duino elegies*. Trans. Stephen Garmey and Jay
Wilson. New York, London: Harper and Row, 1972, pb.

1635 *Duino elegies*. Trans. David Young. New York:
Norton, 1978.

1636 *Elegies of Duino*. Bilingual. Trans. N. Wydenbruck.
Vienna: Amandus Edition, 1948.

RILKE (cont'd).

1637   *Ewald Tragy* (Ewald Tragy). Bilingual. Trans.
        Lola Gruenthal. New York: Twayne Publ.; London:
        Vision Press, 1958.

1638   *From the remains of Count C.W.* (Aus Rainer Maria
        Rilkes Nachlass). Bilingual. Trans. James B.
        Leishman. London: Hogarth Press, 1952; New York:
        British Book Centre, 1953.

1639   *Gym period.* Trans. Carl Niemeyer. In Spender,
        Great German short stories.

1640   *How old Timofei died singing.* In Lange, *Great
        German short novels.*

1641   *Lay of the love and death of Cornet Christoph
        Rilke* (Die Weise von Liebe und Tod des Cornets
        Christoph Rilke). Bilingual. Trans. B.J. Morse.
        Vienna: Amandus Editions, n.d. Cf. 1651.

1642   *The lay of the love and death of Cornet Christoph
        Rilke.* Trans. L. Phillips and S. Schimanski.
        London: Benn, 1948; Hollywood-by-the-sea, Fla.,
        Forest Hills, N.Y.: Transatlantic Arts, 1949.

1643   *Lay of the love and death of Cornet Christoph
        Rilke.* Bilingual. Trans. M.D. Herter Norton.
        New York: Norton, 1959.

1644   *Life of Mary* (Das Marien-Leben). Bilingual.
        Trans. N.K. Cruikshank. Introd. Jethro Bithell.
        London: Oliver and Boyd, 1952.

1645   *Life of the Virgin Mary* (Das Marien-Leben). Trans.
        C.F. MacIntyre. Berkeley, Ca.: University of
        California Press, 1947; Westport, Conn.: Green-
        wood Press, 1972.

RILKE (cont'd).

1646   *The life of the Virgin Mary* (Das Marien-Leben).
Bilingual. Trans. Stephen Spender. London:
Vision Press, 1951; New York: Philosophical
Library, 1952.

1647   *Notebooks of Malte Laurids Brigge* (Die Aufzeich-
nungen des Malte Laurids Brigge). Bilingual.
Trans. M.D. Herter Norton. New York: Norton,
1949, 1964, pb; London: Hogarth Press, 1950;
New York: Putnam, 1958, pb.

1648   *Poems from the Book of Hours* (Stundenbuch). Bilingual. Trans. Babette Deutsch. Norfolk, Conn.:
New Directions, 1941. Cf. 1628.

1649   *Requiem, and other poems.* Trans. James B. Leishman. New York: British Book Centre; London:
Hogarth Press, 1935, 1957.

1650   *Rodin.* Trans. Jessie Lemont and Hans Fransil.
New York: Fine Editions, 1945.

1651   *Song of the life and death of the Cornet Christoph
Rilke* (Die Weise von Liebe und Tod des Cornets
Christoph Rilke). Trans. Howard Strouth. New
York: Heinemann, 1950. Cf. 1641.

1652   *Sonnets of Orpheus* (Sonette an Orpheus). Bilingual.
Trans. J.B. Leishman. London: Hogarth, 1957.

1653   *Sonnets to Orpheus. Duino elegies.* Trans. Jessie
Lemont. New York: Fine Editions, 1945.

1654   *Sonnets to Orpheus* (Sonette an Orpheus). Trans.
C.F. MacIntyre. Berkeley, Ca.: University of
California Press, 1960.

RILKE (cont'd).

1655 *Sonnets to Orpheus.* Trans. M.D. Herter Norton.
New York: Norton, 1942, 1962, pb.

1656 *Sonnets to Orpheus.* Trans. Karl H. Siegler.
Vancouver, B.C.: Talonbooks, 1977.

1657 *Stories of God* (Geschichten vom lieben Gott). Trans.
M.D. Herter Norton. New York: Norton, 1963, pb.

1658 *Visions of Christ: A posthumous cycle of poems.*
Trans. Aaron Kramer. Boulder, Colo.: University
of Colorado Press, 1967.

1659 *The voices* (A selection from 'Buch der Bilder').
Trans. Robert Bly. Denver: Ally Press; Bedford:
Sceptre Press, 1977, 16p.

1660 *Correspondence in verse with Erika Mitterer*
(Briefwechsel in Gedichten mit Erika Mitterer).
Bilingual. Trans. N.K. Cruikshank. Introd. J.B.
Leishman. London: Hogarth Press, 1953.

1661 *His last friendship: Unpublished letters to Mrs.
Eloui Bey.* Trans. W.H. Kennedy. New York: Philosophical Library, 1952.

1662 *Letters of Rainer Maria Rilke.* Trans. J.B. Greene
and M.D. Herter Norton. New York: Norton, 1945-
1948, 2 vols., pb.

1663 *The letters.* Trans. N. Wydenbruck. London: Hogarth Press, 1958.

1664 *The letters of Rainer Maria Rilke and Princess
Marie von Thurn and Taxis.* Trans. N. Wydenbruck.
Ed. Ernst Zinn. London: Hogarth Press; Norfolk,
Conn.: New Directions, 1958.

RILKE (cont'd).

1665 *Letters to a young poet.* Trans. M.D. Herter
Norton. New York: Norton, 1954, 1963, pb.

1666 *Letters to a young poet.* Trans. Reginald Snell.
London: Sidgwick and Jackson, 1955.

1667 *Letters to Benvenuta.* Trans. H. Norden. New York:
Philosophical Library, 1951; London: Hogarth Press,
1953.

1668 *Letters to Frau Gude Nölke during his life in
Switzerland.* Ed. Paul Obermüller. Trans. Violet
M. Macdonald. London: Hogarth Press, 1955.

1669 *Letters to Merline, 1919-1922.* Trans. Violet M.
Macdonald. London: Methuen, 1951.

1670 *Wartime letters of Rainer Maria Rilke, 1914-1921.*
Trans. M.D. Herter Norton. New York: Norton, 1940,
pb.

1671 Selections in: Francke, *The German classics,* XVIII:
Flores, *Anthology of German poetry;* Salinger,
Twentieth-century German verse; Forster, *Penguin
German verse;* Bridgwater, *Twentieth-century Ger-
man verse;* Hamburger, *Modern German poetry;* Ham-
burger, *German poetry 1910-1975;* MacInnes, *A
collection of German verse;* Thomas, *German verse;*
Kaufmann, *Twenty-five German poets;* Deutsch,
Contemporary German poetry; Bithell, *Contemporary
German poetry.*

1672 RINSER, Luise.
Nina (Mitte des Lebens). Trans. Richard and
Clara Winston. Chicago: Regnery, 1956.

RINSER (cont'd).

1673   *Rings of glass* (Die gläsernen Ringe). Trans.
Richard and Clara Winston. Chicago: Regnery, 1958.

1674 ROEHLER, Klaus.
The dignity of night (Die Würde der Nacht). Trans.
John and Necke Mander. In Middleton, *German
writing today*.

1675 ROTH, Joseph.
Flight without end (Die Flucht ohne Ende). Trans.
David Le Vay, in collaboration with Beatrice Mus-
grave. London: Owen, 1977.

1676   *Job* (Hiob). Trans. D. Thompson. New York, 1931.

1677   *The Radetzky march* (Radetzkymarsch). Trans. Eva
Tucker, based on an earlier trans. by Geoffrey
Dunlop. New York, 1933; London: Allen Lane, 1974;
Woodstock, N.Y.: Overlook Press, 1974.

1678   *The silent prophet* (Der stumme Prophet). Trans.
David Le Vay. London: Owen, 1979.

1679 RUTENBORN, Guenter.
The sign of Jonah. Trans. George White. New York:
Nelson, 1960.

1680 SACHS, Nelly.
O the chimneys: Selected poems. Bilingual. Trans.
Michael Hamburger and others. New York: Farrar,
Straus and Giroux, 1967; London: Cape, 1968 (as
Selected poems).

1681   *The seeker, and other poems* (Die Fahrt ins Staub-
lose. Späte Gedichte. Die Suchende). Bilingual.
Trans. Ruth and Matthew Mead and Michael Hamburger.
New York: Farrar, Straus and Giroux, 1970.

1682 SCHAFFNER, Jakob.

   The iron idol. Trans. Amelia von Ende. In
   Francke, *The German classics*, XIX.

1683 SCHAMONI, Ulrich.

   Their fathers' sons. Trans. Michael Bullock.
   London: Barrie and Rockcliff, 1963.

1684 SCHAPER, Edzard.

   The dancing bear (Das Tier). Trans. Norman Denny.
   London: Bodley Head, 1960; New York: Day, 1961.

1685 *Star over the frontier* (Stern über der Grenze).
   Trans. Isabel and Florence McHugh. Baltimore:
   Helicon Press, 1960.

1686 SCHMIDT, Arno.

   The egghead republic (Die Gelehrtenrepublik).
   Trans. Michael Horovitz. London: Boyars, 1979.

1687 From *Die Gelehrtenrepublik*. Trans. Michael
   Horovitz. In Middleton, *German writing today*.

1688 SCHNABEL, Ernst.

   *Story for Icarus; projects, incidents, and con-
   clusions from the life of D., engineer*. Trans.
   J.J. Dunbar. New York: Harcourt, Brace, 1961.

1689 *The voyage home* (Der sechste Gesang). Trans.
   Denver Lindley. London: Gollancz; New York:
   Harcourt, Brace, 1958.

1690 SCHNEIDER, Reinhold.

   The hour of Saint Francis of Assisi (Die Stunde
   des heiligen Franz von Assisi). Trans. James
   Meyer. Chicago: Franciscan Herald, 1963.

SCHNEIDER (cont'd).

1691   *Imperial mission* (Las Casas vor Karl V). Trans.
W. Oden. New York: Gresham Press, 1948.

1692 SCHNITZLER, Arthur.
Little novels (Contains ten short narrative
pieces). Trans. Eric Sutton. New York: Simon
and Schuster, 1929; AMS Press, 1974.

1693   *Vienna 1900: Games with love and death.* Harmondsworth: Penguin, 1973, pb. (Mother and son; The
man of honour; A confirmed bachelor; The spring
sonata).

1694   *Viennese novelettes* (Contains five short narrative
pieces). Introd. Otto P. Schinnerer. New York:
Simon and Schuster, 1931; AMS Press, 1974.

1695   *Anatol* (Anatol). Selections. Trans. W.H.H.
Chambers. In Bates, *German drama*, III.

1696   *Anatol.* Trans. H. Granville-Barker. In
Bentley, *From the modern repertoire*, III.

1697   *Beatrice* (Frau Beate und ihr Sohn). Trans. Agnes
Jacques. New York: Simon and Schuster, 1926;
AMS Press, 1971.

1698   *Casanova's home-coming* (Casanovas Heimfahrt).
Trans. Eden and Cedar Paul. New York: Simon and
Schuster, 1930; New York: Avon, 1948; Citadel,
1949; London: Weidenfeld and Nicolson, 1954;
London: World Distr., 1959, pb. New York: AMS
Press, 1971

1699   *Dance of love* (Reigen). Trans. Keene Wallis. New
York: Award Books, 1965. Cf. 1709-12, 1715, 1721-22.

SCHNITZLER (cont'd).

1700　*Daybreak* (Spiel im Morgengrauen).　Trans. William
A. Drake.　New York: Simon and Schuster, 1927;
AMS Press, 1971.

1701　*Dr. Graesler* (Doktor Gräsler, Badearzt).　Trans.
E.C. Slade.　New York: Simon and Schuster, 1930;
New York: AMS Press, 1971.

1702　*A farewell*.　In Lange, *Great German short novels*.

1703　*The fate of the baron*.　Trans. Eric Sutton.　In
Cerf, *Great German short novels and stories*.

1704　*Flight into darkness* (Flucht in die Finsternis).
Trans. William A. Drake.　New York: Simon and
Schuster, 1931; New York: AMS Press, 1971.

1705　*Fräulein Else* (Fräulein Else).　In Steinhauer,
Twelve German novellas.

1706　*Fräulein Else* (Fräulein Else).　Trans. Robert A.
Simon.　New York: Simon and Schuster, 1925; AMS
Press, 1971.

1707　*The game of love* (Liebelei).　In Corrigan, *Masterpieces of the modern Central European theatre*.

1708　*The green cockatoo* (Der grüne Kakadu).　Trans.
Horace Samuel.　In Francke, *The German classics*, XX.

1709　*La ronde* (Reigen).　Trans. Eric Bentley.　In
Bentley, *The modern theatre*, II.

1710　*La ronde*.　Trans. Frank and Jacqueline Marcus.
London: Harborough Publ., 1959, pb; London: Tandem
Books, 1964.　Originally published as *Merry-go-
round* (1953).

SCHNITZLER (cont'd).

1711   *La ronde.* In Corrigan, *Masterpieces of the modern
Central European theatre.*

1712   *La ronde.* Trans. Carl Richard Mueller. In Corrigan,
The modern theatre. Cf. 1699, 1715, 1721-22.

1713   *Literature.* Trans. A. Coleman. In Francke, *The
German classics*, XX.

1714   *The little comedy and other stories* (Die kleine Ko-
mödie). Trans. various. New York: Ungar, 1977, pb.

1715   *Merry-go-round* (Reigen). Trans. Frank and Jacqueline Marcus. London: Weidenfeld and Nicolson,
1953; New York: British Book Centre, 1954. Cf.
1699, 1709-12, 1721-22.

1716   *The mind in words and actions* (Der Geist im Wort
und der Geist in der Tat). Trans. Robert O. Weiss.
New York: Ungar, 1972.

1717   *My youth in Vienna.* Trans. Catherine Hutter.
New York: Holt, Rinehart and Winston, 1970;
London: Weidenfeld and Nicolson, 1971.

1718   *None but the brave* (Leutnant Gustl). Trans.
Richard L. Simon. New York: Simon and Schuster,
1926; New York: AMS Press, 1971.

1719   *Professor Bernhardi* (Professor Bernhardi). Trans.
Hetty Landstone. New York: Simon and Schuster,
1928; New York: AMS Press, 1971.

1720   *Rhapsody* (Traumnovelle). Trans. Otto P. Schinnerer.
New York: Simon and Schuster, 1927; New York: AMS
Press, 1971.

SCHNITZLER (cont'd).

1721   *Round dance* (Reigen). Trans. Eric Bentley. In Wellwarth, *Themes of drama.*

1722   *Round dance.* Trans. Keene Wallis. In Bentley, *From the modern repertoire*, I. Cf. 1699, 1709-12, 1715.

1723   *The shepherd's pipe, and other stories.* (Die Hirten-flöte, et al.). Trans. O.F. Theis. New York: Brown, 1922; Freeport, N.Y.: Books for Libraries Press, 1970.

1724   *Some day peace will return: Notes on war and peace* (Über Krieg und Frieden). Trans. Robert O. Weiss. New York: Ungar, 1972.

1725   *Theresa* (Therese: Chronik eines Frauenlebens). Trans. William A. Drake. New York: Simon and Schuster, 1928; AMS Press, 1971.

1726   *Viennese idylls.* Trans. Frederick Eisemann. Freeport, N.Y.: Books for Libraries Press, 1973.

1727   and Raoul Auernheimer. *The correspondence of Arthur Schnitzler and Raoul Auernheimer.* Chapel Hill, N.C.: University of North Carolina Press, 1972.

1728   See also: Salinger, *Twentieth-century German verse*; Lamport, *German short stories.*

1729 SCHNURRE, Wolfdietrich.
    See: Newnham, *German short stories.*

1730 SCHOENBERG, Arnold.
    Letters (Ausgewählte Briefe). Trans. Eithne Wilkins and Ernst Kaiser. London: Faber, 1964.

1731 SCHWITTERS, Kurt.

Selections in: Watts, *Three painter-poets*.

1732 SEGHERS, Anna.

The dead stay young (Die Toten bleiben jung).
Boston: Little, Brown; London: Eyre and Spottis-
woode, 1950.

1733 *Revolt of the fishermen of Santa Barbara. A price
on his head* (Der Aufstand der Fischer von Santa
Barbara. Der Kopflohn). Ed. Valerie Stone. Trans.
Jack and Renate Mitchell and Eva Wulff. Berlin:
Seven Seas Publ., 1960; London: Collett, 1961, pb.

1734 *The seventh cross* (Das siebte Kreuz). Trans.
James A. Galson. Boston: Little, Brown, 1942;
New York: Bantam, 1968.

1735 SEIDEL, Ina.

Selections in: Salinger, *Twentieth-century German
verse*.

1736 SORGE, Reinhard.

The beggar (Der Bettler). Trans. Walter H. and
Jacqueline Sokel. In Sokel, *Anthology of German
expressionist drama*.

1737 SPERR, Martin.

Hunting scenes from Lower Bavaria (Jagdszenen aus
Niederbayern). Trans. Christopher Holme. In
Roloff, *The contemporary German theatre*.

1738 *Tales from Landshut* (Landshuter Erzählungen).
Trans. Anthony Vivis. London: Methuen, 1969.

1739 SPITTELER, Carl.

Selections in: Francke, *The German classics*, XIV.

1740 STERNHEIM, Carl.
Scenes from the heroic life of the middle classes;
Five plays. Trans. M.A.L. Brown and others. Ed.
J.M. Ritchie. London: Calder and Boyars, 1970.

1741 *The mask of virtue* (Die Marquise von Arcis).
Adapted by Ashley Dukes. London and New York,
1935.

1742 *The snob* (Der Snob). Trans. Eric Bentley. In
Bentley, *From the modern repertoire*, I.

1743 *The strongbox* (Die Kasette). Trans. Maurice
Edwards and Valerie Reich. In Sokel, *Anthology*
of German expressionist drama.

1744 *The underpants* (Die Hose). Trans. Eric Bentley.
In Bentley, *The modern theatre*, VI.

1745 STRAMM, August.
Twenty two poems. Trans. Patrick Bridgwater.
Wymondham, Leics.: Brewhouse Press, 1969 (lim. ed.).

1746 *Awakening* (Das Erwachen). Trans. J.M. Ritchie.
In Ritchie/Garten, *Seven expressionist plays.*

1747 STRAUSS, Emil.
Mara. Trans. W.G. Howard. In Francke, *The*
German classics, XIX.

1748 STRITTMATTER, Erwin.
Ole Bienkopp (Ole Bienkopp). Trans. Jack and
Renate Mitchell. Berlin: Seven Seas Publ., 1966.

1749 SYLVANUS, Erwin.
Dr. *Korczak and the children* (Korczak und die Kin-
der). Trans. George E. Wellwarth. In Benedikt/
Wellwarth, *Postwar German theatre.*

1750 THOMA, Ludwig.

The girl from India. Trans. Richard Thonger.
In Yuill, *German narrative prose*, II.

1751 *Matt the Holy.* Trans. B.Q. Morgan. In Francke,
The German classics, XIX.

1752 TOLLER, Ernst.

Seven plays. Trans. various. London: Bodley
Head, 1935; New York: Liveright, 1936.

1753 *The blind goddess* (Die blinde Göttin). Trans.
Edward Crankshaw. London, 1934.

1754 *Brokenbrow* (Hinkemann). Trans. V. Mendel.
London, 1926.

1755 *Draw the fires!* (Feuer aus den Kesseln). Trans.
Edward Crankshaw. London, 1935.

1756 *Hinkemann* (Hinkemann). Trans. J.M. Ritchie. In
Ritchie, *Vision and aftermath*. Cf. 1754.

1757 *Hoppla!* (Hoppla, wir leben!). Trans. Herman
Ould. London, 1928.

1758 *Hoppla! Such is life!* Trans. Herman Ould. In
Ulanov, *Makers of the modern theater*.

1759 *The machine wreckers* (Die Maschinenstürmer).
Trans. Ashley Dukes. New York, London, 1923.

1760 *The machine-wreckers.* Trans. Ashley Dukes. In
Moses, *Dramas of modernism*.

1761 *Man and the masses* (Masse Mensch). Trans. Louis
Untermeyer. Garden City, N.Y.: Doubleday, 1924.

1762 *No more peace!* Trans. Edward Crankshaw and W.H.
Auden. London, 1937.

TOLLER (cont'd).

1763   *No more peace!* Trans. Edward Crankshaw and W.H.
       Auden. In Wellwarth, *German drama between the wars.*

1764   *Pastor Hall* (Pastor Hall). Trans. Stephen Spender.
       London, 1939.

1765   *Transfiguration* (Die Wandlung). Trans. Edward
       Crankshaw. In Hatcher, *Modern continental dramas.*

1766   *I was a German: Autobiography* (Eine Jugend in Deutsch-
       land). Trans. Edward Crankshaw. London: Lane, 1934.

1767 TRAKL, Georg.
       Decline: Twelve poems. Trans. Michael Hamburger.
       Saint Ives, Cornwall, Latin Press, 1952.

1768   *Poems.* Bilingual. Ed. and trans. Lucia Getsi.
       Athens, Ohio: Mundus Artium Press, 1973.

1769   *Selected poems.* Bilingual. Trans. Robert Grenier
       and others. Ed. Christopher Middleton. London:
       Cape; New York: Grossmann, 1968.

1770   *Twenty poems.* Bilingual. Trans. James Wright and Ro-
       bert Bly. Madison, Minn.: The Sixties Press, 1961, pb.

1771   Selections in: Flores, *Anthology*; Salinger, *Twentieth
       century German verse*; Forster, *Penguin German verse*;
       Bridgwater, *Twentieth-century German verse*; Ham-
       burger, *Modern German poetry*; Hamburger, *German
       poetry 1910-1975*; Kaufmann, *Twenty-five German poets.*

1772 TUCHOLSKY, Kurt.
       The world is a comedy: A Tucholsky anthology.
       Ed. and trans. Harry Zohn. Cambridge, Mass.:
       Sci-Art Publ., 1957.

TUCHOLSKY (cont'd).

1773   and Walter Hasenclever. *Christopher Columbus*
         (Christoph Columbus). Trans. Max Spalter and
         G.E. Wellwarth. In Wellwarth, *German drama be-*
         tween the wars.

1774   *Deutschland, Deutschland über alles: A picture-*
         book. Trans. Anne Halley. Amherst, Mass.:
         University of Massachusetts Press, 1972.

1775   *What if--? Satirical writings.* Trans. Harry
         Zohn and Karl F. Ross. New York: Funk and
         Wagnall, 1968.

1776 UNRUH, Fritz von.
         Bonaparte (Bonaparte). Trans. E. Björkman. New
         York, 1928.

1777   *The end is not yet: A novel of hate and love.*
         New York: Storm, 1947.

1778   *The saint* (Der Heilige). Trans. W.R. Trask. New
         York: Random House, 1950.

1779 VIEBIG, Clara.
         Burning love. Trans. W.G. Howard. In Francke,
         The German classics, XIX.

1780 WALSER, Martin.
         Plays: Volume 1. London: Calder, 1963. The rabbit
         race, adapted by Ronald Duncan; The detour, trans.
         Richard Grunberger (Eiche und Angora; Der Abstecher).

1781   *After Siegfried's death* (Nach Siegfrieds Tod).
         Trans. Christopher Middleton. In Middleton,
         German writing today.

WALSER, Martin (cont'd).

1782   *Home front* (Zimmerschlacht). Trans. Carole Burden and Christopher Holme. In Roloff, *The contemporary German theater*.

1783   *The Gadarene club* (Ehen in Philippsburg). Trans. Eva Figes. London: Longmans, Green, 1960. Cf. 1784.

1784   *Marriage in Philippsburg* (Ehen in Philippsburg). Norfolk, Conn.: New Directions, 1961. Cf. 1783.

1785   *The unicorn* (Das Einhorn). Trans. Barrie Ellis-Jones. London: Calder and Boyars, 1971.

1786 WALSER, Robert.
Jakob von Gunten: A novel (Jakob von Gunten). Trans. Christopher Middleton. Austin, Tex.: University of Texas Press, 1969.

1787   *A village tale.* Trans. Christopher Middleton. In Spender, *Great German short stories*.

1788   *The walk, and other stories* (Der Spaziergang). Trans. Christopher Middleton. London: Calder, 1957.

1789 WASSERMANN, Jakob.
Alexander in Babylon (Der Wendekreis). New York: Crown Publ.; Chicago: Ziff-Davis, 1949.

1790   *Caspar Hauser, the enigma of a century* (Caspar Hauser). Trans. Caroline Newton. New York: Liveright Publ., 1928, 1963; Blauvelt, N.Y.: Rudolf Steiner Publs., 1973.

1791   *Clarissa Mirabel.* Trans. Julia Franklin. In Francke, *The German classics*, XX.

1792   *Doctor Kerkhoven* (Etzel Andergast). Trans. Cyrus Brooks. New York: Liveright, 1932, 1965.

WASSERMANN (cont'd).

1793   *Lukardis*. Trans. Lewis Galantiere. In Cerf,
        Great German short novels and stories.

1794   *Lukardis*. Trans. Lewis Galantiere. In Pick,
        German stories and tales.

1795   *The Maurizius case* (Der Fall Maurizius). Trans.
        Caroline Newton. New York: Liveright Publ., 1929,
        1960; New York: Pyramid Books, 1964, pb.

1796   *Wedlock* (Laudin und die seinen). Trans. Ludwig
        Lewisohn. New York: Pyramid Books, 1964, pb.

1797   *The world's illusion* (Christian Wahnschaffe).
        Trans. L. Lewisohn. New York, 1920, 1930.

1798 WEDEKIND, Frank.
        Five tragedies of sex. Trans. F. Fawcett and
        Stephen Spender. New York: Theatre Arts Books;
        London: Vision Press, 1952.

1799   *The Lulu plays.* Trans. Carl R. Mueller. Green-
        wich, Conn.: Fawcett, 1967. (Earth spirit; Pan-
        dora's box; Death and the devil).

1800   *The Lulu plays, and other sex tragedies.* Trans.
        Stephen Spender. London: Vision, 1952; Calder
        and Boyars, 1972. (Earth spirit; Pandora's box;
        Death and the devil; Castle Wetterstein).

1801   *The burning of Egliswyl.* In Lange, *Great German
        short novels.*

1802   *The court singer* (Der Kammersänger). Trans. A.W.
        Boesche. In Francke, *The German classics*, XX.
        Cf. 1812.

WEDEKIND (cont'd).

1803   *Earth spirit* (Erdgeist). Trans. S.A. Eliot. New
York, 1914.

1804   *King Nicolo, or Such is life* (König Nicolo, oder
So ist das Leben). Trans. Martin Esslin. In
Esslin, *The genius of the German theater.*

1805   *The marquis of Keith* (Der Marquis von Keith).
Trans. Beatrice Gottlieb. In Bentley, *From the
modern repertoire*, II.

1806   *The marquis of Keith.* Trans. Beatrice Gottlieb.
In Block, *Masters of modern drama.*

1807   *The marquis of Keith.* Trans. Carl Richard
Mueller. In Corrigan, *Masterpieces of the modern
German theatre.*

1808   *The marquis of Keith.* Trans. Carl Richard Mueller.
In Corrigan, *The modern theatre.*

1809   *Pandora's box* (Die Büchse der Pandora). Trans.
S.A. Eliot. New York, 1918.

1810   *Spring awakening* (Frühlings Erwachen). Trans.
Tom Osborn. London: Calder and Boyars, 1969.

1811   *Spring's awakening.* In Bentley, *The modern
theatre*, VI.

1812   *The tenor* (Der Kammersänger). Trans. Andre Tridon.
In Gassner, *A treasury of the theatre*, II. Cf. 1802.

1813   WEINHEBER, Josef.
Selections in: Salinger, *Twentieth-century German
verse.*

1814   WEISENBORN, Günther.

The fury (Die Furie). Trans. Richard and Clarissa
Graves. London: Hutchinson, 1956.

1815   WEISS, Peter.

Bodies and shadows: Two novels (Der Schatten des
Körpers des Kutschers; Gespräch der drei Gehenden).
Trans. E.B. Garside and Rosemarie Waldrop. New
York: Delacorte, 1969. Cf. 1816.

1816   *The conversation of the three walkers, and The
shadow of the coachman's body* (Gespräch der drei
Gehenden; Der Schatten des Körpers des Kutschers).
Trans. S.M. Cupitt. London: Calder and Boyars,
1972. Cf. 1815.

1817   *Discourse on Vietnam* (Diskurs über . . . Viet Nam).
Trans. Geoffrey Skelton. New York: Atheneum Press,
1970; London: Calder and Boyars, 1971, pb. Cf. 1828.

1818   *Exile: A novel* (Abschied von den Eltern. Fluchtpunkt). Trans. E.B. Garside, Alastair Hamilton,
and Christopher Levenson. New York: Delacorte
Press, 1968. Cf. 1822.

1819   *How Mr. Mockinpott was cured of his suffering*
(Wie dem Herrn Mockinpott das Leiden ausgetrieben
wird). Trans. Christopher Holme. In Roloff,
The contemporary German theater.

1820   *The investigation* (Die Ermittlung). Trans. Alexander Gross. London: Calder and Boyars, 1966.

1821   *The investigation.* Trans. Jon Swan and Ulu Gros-
bard. New York: Atheneum, 1966; Pocket Books,
1967, pb.

WEISS (cont'd).

1822   *Leavetaking. Vanishing point* (Abschied von den
Eltern. Fluchtpunkt). Trans. Christopher Levenson.
New York: Harcourt, Brace, 1962; London: Calder
and Boyars, 1966. Cf. 1818.

1823   *Marat/Sade* (Die Verfolgung und Ermordung Jean
Paul Marats). Trans. Geoffrey Skelton and Adrian
Mitchell. London: Calder, 1965; New York: Atheneum,
1966; Pocket Books, 1966; London: Calder and Boyars,
1969.

1824   *My place* (Meine Ortschaft). Trans. Christopher
Middleton. In Middleton, *German writing today.*

1825   *Notes on the cultural life of the democratic
republic of Viet Nam* (Notizen zum kulturellen
Leben der Demokratischen Republik Viet Nam).
London: Calder and Boyars, 1971.

1826   *The tower* (Der Turm). Trans. Michael Benedikt
and Michel Heine. In Benedikt/Wellwarth, *Postwar
German theatre.*

1827   *Trotsky in exile* (Trotzki in Exil). Trans. Geoffrey Skelton. London: Methuen, 1971, pb; New
York: Atheneum, 1972; New York: Pocket Books, 1973.

1828   *Two plays* (Gesang vom Lusitanischen Popanz. Diskurs über Vietnam). Trans. Leo Baxandall, Geoffrey Skelton. New York: Atheneum, 1970.

1829   WELLERSHOFF, Dieter.
A beautiful day (Ein schöner Tag). Trans. Dorothea Oppenheimer. New York: Harper and Row, 1971.

1830 WERFEL, Franz.

Poems. Trans. Edith Abercrombie Snow. Princeton, N.J.: Princeton University Press, 1945.

1831 *Between heaven and earth* (Zwischen oben und unten). Trans. Maxim Newmark. New York: Hutchinson, 1947; Freeport, N.Y.: Books for Libraries Press, 1971.

1832 *Embezzled heaven* (Der veruntreute Himmel). Trans. Moray Firth. New York: Dell, 1959, pb; New York: Popular Library, 1967.

1833 *The eternal road* (Der Weg der Verheissung). Trans. L. Lewisohn. New York, 1936; London, 1937.

1834 *The forty days of Musa Dagh* (Die vierzig Tage des Musa Dagh). Trans. Geoffrey Dunlop (1934). New York: Pocket Books, 1962, pb. New York: Viking, 1967.

1835 *Goat song* (Bocksgesang). Trans. R. Langner, New York, 1936.

1836 *Jacobowsky and the colonel* (Jacobowsky und der Oberst). Trans. S.N. Behrman. New York, 1944.

1837 *Jacobowsky and the colonel*. Adapted by S.N. Behrman. In Gassner, *Twenty best European plays*.

1838 *Juarez and Maximilian* (Juarez und Maximilian). Trans. R. Langner, New York, 1926.

1839 *The Pascarella family* (Die Geschwister von Neapel). Trans. D.F. Tait. New York: Simon and Schuster, 1932.

1840 *Paul among the Jews* (Paulus unter den Juden). Trans. P. Leverthoff. London, 1928, 1943.

WERFEL (cont'd).

1841   *The song of Bernadette* (Das Lied von Bernadette).
        Trans. Ludwig Lewisohn. New York: Viking Press,;
        London: H. Hamilton, 1942; London: Pan Books, 1950,
        pb; New York Pocket Books, 1953, pb; New York:
        Viking Press, 1956, pb; London: Collins, 1958,
        pb; St. Albans: Mayflower, 1977, pb.

1842   *Star of the unborn* (Stern der Ungeborenen). Trans.
        Gustave O. Arlt. New York: Viking, 1946.

1843   *Verdi.* Trans. Helen Jessiman. New York: Allen,
        Towne and Heath, 1925, 1947.

1844   See also: Salinger, *Twentieth-century German verse*;
        Kaufmann, *Twenty-five German poets.*

1845   WIECHERT, Ernst.
        The earth is our heritage (Die Jeromin-Kinder).
        Trans. R. Maxwell. London: Nevill, 1950; Westport,
        Conn.: Associated Booksellers, 1955.

1846   *Forest of the dead* (Der Totenwald). Trans. Ursula
        Stechow. New York: Greenberg, 1947.

1847   *The girl and the ferryman* (Die Magd des Jürgen
        Doskocil). Trans. Eithne Wilkins and Ernst
        Kaiser. New York: Pilot, 1947.

1848   *Missa sine nomine* (Missa sine nomine). Trans. Marie
        Heynemann and Margery B. Ledward. London: Nevill,
        1953; New York: British Book Centre, 1954; New York:
        Macmillan, 1959 (Under title *Tidings*). Cf. 1851.

1849   *The poet and his time: Three addresses* (Der Dichter
        und die Zeit). Trans. Irene Taeuber. Hinsdale,
        Ill,: Regnery, 1948.

WIECHERT, Ernst (cont'd).

1850   *The simple life* (Das einfache Leben). Trans. Marie
        Heynemann. London: Nevill, 1954.

1851   *Tidings* (Missa sine nomine). Trans. Marie Heyne-
        mann and Margery B. Ledward. New York: Macmillan,
        1959. Cf. 1848.

1852   See also: Salinger, *Twentieth-century German verse.*

1853 WIENS, Paul.
        Selections in: Deicke, *Time for dreams.*

1854 WOLF, Christa.
        Divided heaven (Der geteilte Himmel). Trans.
        Joan Becker. Berlin: Seven Seas Publ., 1965.

1855   *The quest for Christa T* (Nachdenken über Christa T).
        Trans. Christopher Middleton. New York: Farrar,
        Straus and Giroux, 1970; London: Hutchinson, 1971.

1856   *The reader and the writer: Essays, sketches,
        memories* (Lesen und Schreiben). Trans. Joan
        Becker. New York: International, 1978, pb.

1857 WOLF, Friedrich.
        The sailors of Cattaro (Die Matrosen von Cattaro).
        Trans. K. Wallis. New York, London, 1935.

1858 WOLFSKEHL, Karl.
        1933, A poem sequence (Die Stimme spricht). Trans.
        Carol North Valhope and Ernst Morwitz. New York:
        Schocken, 1947.

1859 ZAHN, Ernst.
        Stephen the smith. Trans. Katharine Royce. In
        Francke, *The German classics*, XIX.

1860 ZUCKMAYER, Carl.

The captain of Köpenick (Der Hauptmann von Köpenick)
Trans. John Mortimer. London: Methuen, 1971.

1861 *The captain of Köpenick.* Trans. Carl R. Mueller.
In Wellwarth, *German drama between the wars.*

1862 *The captain of Köpenick.* Trans. D. Portman.
London, 1932.

1863 *Carnival confession* (Die Fastnachtsbeichte).
Trans. John and Necke Mander. London: Methuen,
1961.

1864 *The devil's general* (Des Teufels General). Trans.
Ingrid G. Gilbert and William F. Gilbert. In
Block, *Masters of modern drama.*

1865 *Love story.* Trans. Sheila Rooke. In Yuill,
German narrative prose, II.

1866 *A part of myself* (Als wär's ein Stück von mir).
Trans. Richard and Clara Winston. London: Secker
and Warburg; New York: Harcourt Brace Jovanovich,
1970.

1867 ZWEIG, Arnold.

The axe of Wandsbek (Das Beil von Wandsbek).
Trans. Eric Sutton. London: Hutchinson, 1948.

1868 *A bit of blood, and other stories.* Berlin: Seven
Seas Publ.; London: Collet's, 1959.

1869 *The case of Sergeant Grischa* (Der Streit um den
Sergeanten Grischa). Trans. Eric Sutton. New York:
1928; London: Hutchinson, 1947, 1961, pb; Harrisburg
Pa.: Stackpole Books, 1970.

ZWEIG, Arnold (cont'd).

1870   *The parcel.* Trans. Eric Sutton. In Cerf, *Great German short novels and stories.*

1871   *The time is ripe* (Die Zeit ist reif). Trans. Kenneth Bannerji and Michael Wharton. London: Gibbs and Phillips, 1962.

1872   ZWEIG, Stefan.
Kaleidoscope one (stories and novelettes). Trans. Eden and Cedar Paul. London: Cassell, 1950, 1962.

1873   *Kaleidoscope two* (stories and novelettes). Trans. B.W. Huebsch, and Eden and Cedar Paul. London: Cassell, 1951, 1959.

1874   *Stories and legends.* Trans. Eden and Cedar Paul, and Constantine Fitzgibbon. London: Cassell, 1955.

1875   *Amok* (Amok). Trans. Eden and Cedar Paul. In Cerf, *Great German short novels and stories.* Cf. 1888.

1876   *Balzac.* Trans. W. and D. Rose. New York: Viking, 1946; New York: Doubleday, 1948, pb.

1877   *Beware of pity* (Ungeduld des Herzens). Trans. P. and T. Blewitt. London: Cassell, 1939, 1961; Chester Springs, Pa.: Dufour, 1965.

1878   *Emile Verhaeren.* Trans. Jethro Bithell. Freeport, N.Y.: Books for Libraries Press, 1970.

1879   *Erasmus of Rotterdam.*Trans. Eden and Cedar Paul. New York: Viking Press, 1956, pb.

1880   *Erasmus. The right to heresy.* Trans. Eden and Cedar Paul. London: Cassell, 1951.

ZWEIG, Stefan (cont'd).

1881   *Jeremiah* (Jeremias). Trans. Eden and Cedar Paul.
New York, 1922, London, 1929.

1882   *Joseph Fouché*. Trans. Eden and Cedar Paul.
London: Cassell, 1948, pb.

1883   *Marie Antoinette*. Trans. Eden and Cedar Paul.
London: Cassell, 1953.

1884   *Mary, Queen of Scotland and the Isles*. Trans.
Eden and Cedar Paul. London, 1950; New York:
Lancer, 1971, pb.

1885   *Passion and pain* (stories and novelettes). Trans.
Eden and Cedar Paul. London, 1924; Freeport,
N.Y.: Books for Libraries Press, 1971.

1886   *The queen of Scots*. Trans. Eden and Cedar Paul.
London: Cassell, 1950.

1887   *Right to heresy. Castellio against Calvin*. Trans.
Eden and Cedar Paul. Boston: Beacon Press, 1951.

1888   *The royal game. Amok. Letter from an unknown
woman* (Schachnovelle; Amok; Brief einer Unbekannten).
Trans. B.W. Huebsch, Eden and Cedar Paul. New York:
Viking Press, 1944, 1961, pb.

1889   *The tide of fortune: Twelve historical miniatures*.
Trans. Eden and Cedar Paul. London: Cassell, 1955
(1940).

1890   *Volpone*. Trans. Ruth Langner. In Gassner, *Twenty
best European plays*.

1891   *Stefan and Friderike Zweig: Their correspondence,
1912-1942*. Trans. Henry G. Alsberg and Erna
MacArthur. New York: Hastings, 1954.

ZWEIG, Stefan (cont'd).

1892   *World of yesterday: An autobiography* (Die Welt
        von gestern). Introd. Harry Zohn. Lincoln, Nebr.:
        University of Nebraska Press, 1964, pb.

1893   ZWERENZ, Gerhard.

        Little Peter in war and peace (Casanova, oder Der
        kleine Herr in Krieg und Frieden). Trans. William
        Whitman. New York: Grove Press, 1970; London:
        Cape, 1971; St. Albans: Panther, 1975, pb.

1894   *Remembrance day* (Heldengedenktag). London:
        Hutchinson; New York: Dutton, 1966.

Index of Authors

The index of authors includes every author and—in the case of anonymous works—title represented by a main entry. It does not include authors listed as being contained in collections in section I unless they are also represented by a main entry.

Index of Translators

Asterisked items refer to the collections in section
I, which in turn contain cross-references to the main
author entries.

Behler, Ernst, 837

Behn, Harry, 1631

Behrman, S.N., 1836-37

Beissel, Henry, 941, 942, 1120

Bell, C.H., 155, 232

Bell, C.W., 867

Bell, Clara, 774

Bell, Ernest, 379, 381-82, 384

Benedikt, Michael, *2, 1005, 1207, 1252, 1461, 1826

Bennett, E.N., *4, 496, 506, 688, 726, 895

Bentley, Eric, 410, 477-78, 968, 1016-17, 1022-23, 1025-30, 1033, 1037-39, 1032, 1045, 1051-54, 1056, 1058-59, 1067-70, 1072, 1709, 1721, 1742, 1744

Bentley, Maja, 1025, 1056

Berger, John, 1040, 1057

Bergmann, Sonja, 1148

Betts, Frank, 229

Biermann, Berthold, 354

Bithell, Jethro, *11, *12, 1878

Björkman, E., 1776

Black, John, 835

Black, Kitty, 1333

Blades, William, 118

Blakney, R.B., 123, 127

Bland, C.S., 113

Blewitt, Phyllis and Trevor, 1119, 1877

Bly, Robert, 1659, 1770

Boesche, A.W., 1802

Boetcher-Joeres, Ruth-Ellen, 577

Bogan, Louise, 269, 330, 1379

Bonacina, C.M.R., 1495

Bone, E., 1454

Boney, E.E., 1630

Bostock, Anna, 1042, 1057

Bowles, Patrick, 983, 1139-40

Bowman, Derek, 246

Boyd, Ernest, 1515, 1518

Boylan, R.D., 266-67

Boylton, R.D., 327

Bozman, M.M., 392, 802

Branscombe, Peter, 625

Bremer, S.H., 1024

Bridgwater, Patrick, *14, 1385, 1745

Broch de Rothermann, H.F., 1079

Broicher, Daisy, *16

Brooks, Cyrus, 930, 1128, 1183-85, 1187, 1386, 1792

Brown, M.A.L., 1740

Brownell, J., 825

Brownjohn, J.M., 1446, 1438, 1452-53

Bryan, Florence, 809

Bryant, H., 458

Buehne, S.Z., 157, 1469

Delffs, Sofie, 830-31

Delmer, F.S., 1192

Denny, Norman, 1684

Dent, Anthony, 377

Deutsch, Babette, *29, 1648

Dickens, D.B., 766

Donald, M.B., 691

Drake, W.A., 1182, 1700, 1704, 1725

Duckworth, Elizabeth, 1420,

Dukes, Ashley, 1087, 1429-1432, 1588, 1741, 1759-1760

Dulcken, H.W., 446

Dunbar, J.J., 1688

Duncan, Ronald, 1780

Dunlop, Geoffrey, 466, 1290, 1296, 1307, 1677, 1834

Dvoretzky, Edward, 371

Earle, J.R., 108

Eaves, T.C.D., 336

Edwards, Maurice, 546-47, 1489, 1743

Eisemann, Frederick, 1726

Eitzen, A.E.W., 1579

Elias, J.A., 415

Eliot, S.A., 214-15, 1803, 1809

Ellis, W.A., 906

Ellis-Jones, Barrie, 1785

Ellistone, J., 106-7

Emerson, J., 582

Ende, Amelia von, 1682

Enzensberger, Hans Magnus, 1153

Esslin, Martin, 747, 944-945, 1022, 1804

Esslin, Renata, 944-45

Evans, C. de B., 122

F., P., Gent., 135

F., R., Gent., 117

Fabry, Joseph, 784

Fairley, Barker, 272, 610, 633

Falk, Orson, 325

Fawcett, F., 1798

Feiner, Alfred, 1574

Feise, Ernst, 626

Figes, Eva, 1783

Findlay, Paul, 1217, 1221

Firchow, E.S., 130

Firchow, Peter, 839

Firth, Moray, 1172, 1832

Fitzgerald, Edward, 857

Fitzgibbon, Constantine, 1228, 1230, 1629, 1874

Fleishman, M., 641

Folkers, G.F., 766

Forster, J.R., 861

Forster, Leonard, *35, 114, 247

Fowkes, R.A., 378

Franck, Frederick, 98

Franklin, Julia, 503, 1791

Freeman, M.B., 170

McHugh, Isabel and Florence, 1387, 1492-93, 1685

MacInnes, Isabel, *51

MacIntyre, C.F., 286-87, 1622, 1633, 1645, 1654

MacKendrick, John, 482

Mackenzie, K.R.H., 133

Mackintosh, H.R., 841

MacNeice, Louis, 275, 288

McNeil, Jean, 826

Magoun, F.P., Jr., 131, 571

Mahlendorf, Ursula, 965

Mainland, W.F., 427

Mander, John and Necke, 1674, 1863

Manheim, Ralph, 574, 812 923, 925, 932, 1060, 1238, 1242-45, 1248, 1250, 1251, 1254-55, 1264-65, 1272-73, 1274a, 1287, 1289, 1298, 1302, 1305, 1311-12, 1318, 1323, 1509-12, 1593, 1607, 1609

Marcus, Frank and Jacqueline, 1710, 1715

Marshall, B., 883-84

Martin, Theodore, 276, 429-431

Marx, Olga, 1095, 1097, 1223, 1494

Mathers, S.L.M., 173

Maurer, Karl, 663, 1466

Mautner, Fritz, 389-90

Maxwell, James, 470

Maxwell, R., 1845

Mayer, Elizabeth, 269, 313, 330, 863-64, 1379

Mayer, H., 855

Mayer, Peter, 1152

Mead, Ruth and Matthew, 966, 971, 974-75, 1681

Mellish, Joseph, 410

Meltzer, C.H., 593-94

Mendel, Arthur, 245

Mendel, S., 581

Mendel, V., 1754

Mendelssohn, Peter de, 1438

Menzies, Lucy, 182

Meyer, James, 1690

Michaelis-Jena, Ruth, 572, 1161

Middleton, Christopher, *42, 667, 782, 950, 1106, 1240-41, 1246-1247, 1592, 1781, 1786-1788, 1824, 1855

Mierow, C.C., 198

Millar, J., 866

Miller, T.A., 560

Milnes, Humphrey, 943

Milroy, Vivian, 1596

Mitchell, Adrian, 1823

Mitchell, Jack, *28

Mitchell, Jack and Renate, 1733, 1748

Molinaro, Ursule, 1306, 1373, 1375-76, 1506

Mood, J.J.L., 1619